CHORDS of STRENGTH

CHORDS OF STRENGTH

DAVID ARCHULETA

WITH
MONICA HAIM

A MEMOIR OF SOUL, SONG,
AND THE POWER OF PERSEVERANCE

A CELEBRA BOOK

Celebra
Published by New American Library, a division of
Penguin Group (USA) Inc., 375 Hudson Street,
New York, New York 10014, USA
Penguin Group (Canada), 90 Eglinton Avenue East, Suite 700, Toronto,
Ontario M4P 2Y3, Canada (a division of Pearson Penguin Canada Inc.)
Penguin Books Ltd., 80 Strand, London WC2R 0RL, England
Penguin Ireland, 25 St. Stephen's Green, Dublin 2,
Ireland (a division of Penguin Books Ltd.)
Penguin Group (Australia), 250 Camberwell Road, Camberwell, Victoria 3124,
Australia (a division of Pearson Australia Group Pty. Ltd.)
Penguin Books India Pvt. Ltd., 11 Community Centre, Panchsheel Park,
New Delhi - 110 017, India
Penguin Group (NZ), 67 Apollo Drive, Rosedale, North Shore 0632,
New Zealand (a division of Pearson New Zealand Ltd.)
Penguin Books (South Africa) (Pty.) Ltd., 24 Sturdee Avenue,
Rosebank, Johannesburg 2196, South Africa

Penguin Books Ltd., Registered Offices:
80 Strand, London WC2R 0RL, England

Published by Celebra, an imprint of New American Library,
a division of Penguin Group (USA) Inc.

First Printing, June 2010
10 9 8 7 6 5 4 3 2

LIBRARY OF CONGRESS CATALOGING-IN-PUBLICATION DATA:

Archuleta, David, 1990–
Chords of strength: a memoir of soul, song, and the power of perseverance/David Archuleta.
  p. cm.
ISBN 978-0-451-23018-8
1. Archuleta, David, 1990– 2. Singers—United States—Biography. I. Haim, Monica. II. Title.
ML420.A738A3 2010
782.42164092—dc22 2009053837
[B]

Set in ITC Giovanni
Designed by Pauline Neuwirth

Printed in the United States of America

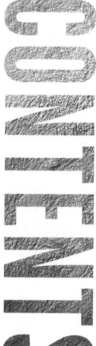

v

To anyone who believes in the power of a dream
and all the possibilities . . .

"I have no idea why I'm doing this, but I know I need to be doing it for some reason."

That was the last entry in my old journal, which I wrote during *American Idol* auditions. I was finally home for the holidays in 2008, hanging out with a friend and going through a bunch of my old stuff when I came across my old journal. I had written on and off over the previous several years about school and friends, and questions about the future and what I was going to do with my life. There was a gap of several months between my last two entries, and the very last one was right before I went to Hollywood the week of *American Idol's* seventh season.

It was November of 2007 when I was still sixteen and in my junior year at Murray High. I had written about how nervous I was to be auditioning for the show and quite sure it wouldn't be too long until I would be booted off and back home and I really had no expectation about what might happen next.

As I read and thought about the events since that last time I had written in my journal, I was a little disappointed with myself. I thought about how I was the only person who really knew my side of the story, of how I really felt when all of this was going on. I saw that back then I was writing about music quite a bit and saying that I really wanted to do something with music but I wasn't sure how I was supposed to do it. It really amazed me when I thought back and tried to put myself back into the state of mind I was in when I had written each entry, and kept thinking, "Wow, you had no idea what was going to happen in the next few years, couple of years, or next year," depending on when the entry was made. I felt bad that I hadn't written down more of what I went through, especially because I hadn't written anything at all during the entire 2008 year while I was on *American Idol*, or the following Top 10 tour and the events surrounding the recording of my first single and making of my first album, all life changing events.

So I made the decision right there in my room that I would make a New Year's resolution to write in my journal at least once a week from then on, even though I thought there was no way I'd be able to keep it going because I hated writing, which is why I couldn't keep it up with that old journal in the first place. Then I thought, I get interviewed all the time and several of my incredibly amazing fans have made very detailed scrapbooks about my life. Did I want to rely on everyone else

No one can see your life the way you see it.

to tell my story of how I started, where I came from and who I am? People were keeping track of me, but no one really had my own story. No one knew what was going on in my mind before people knew my name. I was thinking, man, when I have my kids in the future, I don't want them to rely on what everyone else thought about me. While I hope that people think good things about me and that I left a good name for my family and myself, I want them to hear my story from me in my own words. No one can see your life the way you see it. Not only did I realize at that point the importance of writing in my journal, but also, like I did with singing, how important it is to share it with the most important people in my life: my family, friends and my fans.

So that is the long explanation of why I said yes when I was asked to write a book. Writing in my journal has helped me more than almost anything else I've been doing because it has helped me organize my thoughts and understand what is most important to me, and to think about how I can make sure I keep on track with my personal priorities.

I would have never imagined just over two years ago that I would be recording albums, touring all over the world, writing a book, speaking in front of youth groups and other large audiences, raising awareness for several worthy causes; things that I never believed I would be able to do, let alone have the courage to do them. I remember thinking about when I was too shy, and I hated the sound of my voice, and when doctors told me I might not ever be able to sing again. Back then I was ready to make music a hobby and think about becoming a dentist or a doctor. There I was a few years later, and a world away, reading that journal and first thinking, *Wow! I can't believe I'm actually doing what I dreamed about, and then some.*

I had to overcome many fears to do almost anything I do in public today including singing, speaking in public and, now, having to write a book. When I started singing, as much as I loved it, I had serious issues with my own voice. Even when people would tell me I had a nice voice, I thought they were just being nice because I was a little kid. If someone were to record it and play it back, I would freak out and run out of the room because I couldn't stand my voice. I hated it! I thought I sounded so strange. But I knew one thing: I still loved singing so much that I loved the way it made me feel more than I hated listening to myself, if that makes sense.

I remember the first talent show I did was the Utah Talent Competition when I was ten. I was so afraid to go onstage. I couldn't believe I was doing it. I kept asking, "Why am I doing this?" While I was backstage, I had a panic attack. I was hyperventilating. I remember everyone backstage saying, "You don't have to go on if you don't want to." It was embarrassing! Five minutes before I had to go on, I said to myself I could do it, and I just got up there and sang. I ended up winning the kid's division. I just couldn't believe it. The audience was so supportive. I think they realized how scared and nervous I was because I was shaking so much. That was the first time I had overcome my fear of singing in such a big way that I started to realize how many great things could happen by confronting the things that scare you most.

Sometimes you have to face your fears. Even though I used to fear singing, I went ahead and put myself out there until I started to gain confidence and gradually my fear went away. Same with speaking. I used to dread doing interviews and having to answer questions, and definitely would have never thought I could speak in front of a large crowd of people. I know it was something I needed to face head-on.

This book is supposed to be about persevering and following your dreams, so I ask myself, "What does it mean to follow your dreams?" Well, it's your desire to accomplish something that you really want to do even if it seems difficult. It's, "Well, that something will probably only ever exist in my dreams. That can never happen in reality." But then it's like "Well, why not! I mean, if it's something you really have a desire to do and you feel like it's a good thing, it may seem difficult to do, but you just have to take those first little steps."

I ran cross country for my high school track team when I was in ninth and tenth grades, but during and after *Idol* and touring, I got out of my running routine. So one thing I told myself was that when I got home from tour, I needed to start running again. It was always those moments when my alarm was blaring at me at seven a.m., and I was still dead tired and just didn't feel like getting up that I would notice a little light coming into my room and even though I felt so warm and cozy in my bed, I'd tell myself, "David, if you don't get up, you'll be disappointing yourself. You'll be lying to yourself. You need to get up."

And after a few minutes of internal struggle, I'd get up. And I'd force myself to stretch and go outside and run and once I was running, I wondered why it was so hard to get going in the first place, when the air felt so fresh and my mind was free to think and wonder and figure out what was going on in that spacey head of mine.

That's one of the things I've learned so far in my just over nineteen years. If you want to get better at something, you need to start in the first place even when you don't feel like it and sometimes you need to trust those around you because they may see something in you that you can't see. You need to have a little bit of trust, and a little bit of faith. You also have to decide what the first step is and then stick to it. It's like "Oh well, there's no guarantee I'll ever be good at that" or "I'm just not very good. Why would I think I can actually get better?" and so it's easier to just avoid doing it and try to rationalize it away—kind of like how I have felt about trying to write a book when I have never imagined doing something like this before.

So here I am struggling away trying to write out these pages and you're all my witnesses that I am trying to overcome something here that is terrifying to me, and I hope I'm able to share something that will be of value to you in some way as you are reading this. It really can be difficult to take that first step sometimes because we're fighting this current of fear that's pushing us back. If you really have the desire, if you feel like "Yes, I want to do that," even if it is a hard path to take, even if it has a lot of resistance with big hills and rocks and trees and you can get scratches, and you can trip and fall, and you can get hurt. I think that's what makes us grow the most. It's like when you exercise: The more you do it, the stronger you feel and the easier it gets. And even the soreness the next day really feels great! It's working through the resistance that makes us learn in our lives. So when you get to the end of the path, you have all those bruises and cuts and you can see that you had a difficult time getting to where you are now; but at the same time, you can say, "You know what? I was willing to take that path even if it wasn't the easiest path to take and look where I am now compared to where I was before I started!"

You just have to trust yourself. You have to trust in God. You have to decide, "Yes, I want to do this," and then you have to have the faith and courage to do it. And that's what I want to say here.

My road has definitely come with many bumps and bruises. I had been on *Star Search* when I was twelve and was invited back a year later for what would be the show's final season. After a series of health issues, I was diagnosed with vocal paralysis. Surgery was one option, but it could ruin my voice forever and therapy was the only other option, but with no guarantees. I thought this might be the end of singing for me. Therapy would take one to two years. I couldn't even get through a couple of songs. How was I supposed to be a singer? I went back to my regular life as a teenager and put singing on the back burner. I later got a job and started moving past my dream until *American Idol* auditions came back around. All of my friends and family encouraged me to do it and I thought they were all crazy. Then I thought, "Maybe I should?" As soon as the possibility crept into my head I couldn't get it out. Maybe it was a good idea, but maybe not. I just wasn't sure. I knew only one thing to do, pray. I believed in prayer, but wasn't sure it was appropriate to pray about whether God would care about me wanting to try out for a TV show, but I figured, why not? I knew I had to ask, so I did. And I got an answer. It was: Yes, I should do it.

So I knew that it was something that was right for me to do and I figured, "Even if I don't get past the first round, it couldn't hurt. I'm sure it would be fun and maybe I would learn something from it." I realized that even though I wasn't very confident that I could do it, I knew my family, my friends, and God were behind me. For me, that was enough to keep myself moving forward. My family and friends have always inspired me and supported me to become more than I believed I was capable of.

Right now, I feel so fortunate and blessed to be doing what I am doing with my life. You could say I am living my dream in many ways, but I still look forward to all the new experiences and challenges that lie ahead. In just the last few months I have had some incredible opportunities, which I could have never imagined just a few short years ago. It is hard to believe I am in the middle of working on my third album, and was able to visit Asia, the UK and tour most of the United States throughout last year. I was able to record a Christmas album, which meant so much to me, and then go on a Christmas tour, and even had the privilege of performing with a full orchestra playing new arrangements of both my pop and Christmas songs. I have been able to help with the Haiti Disaster Relief telethon in Hollywood as well as the Spanish language version of "We Are the World" project in Miami—so many other events that I can't begin to list them all. And best of all, I've been able to meet some incredible people along the way from so many different states and countries, and all of this doing something that I love so much, getting to share the gift of music!

I have been so fortunate to have been encouraged and inspired throughout my life by people who cared enough about me to be there when I doubted my own abilities, and I've learned that when I exercise some faith and take the first steps, that usually, somehow, things seem to work out. I hope that through this book as I share some of my experiences and challenges that I've faced, that you can perhaps feel the desire and belief that you can also overcome your fears and go after your dreams.

PURE BEGINNINGS

"It is our choices that show what we truly are, far more than our abilities."

—J. K. ROWLING

I spent the first six years of my life in Florida. Maybe that's why I like warm weather better. It was a sticky heat, filling my childhood with scurrying lizards and duck-egg hunts. My sister Claudia and I used to poke around the yard of our first townhome, looking for duck eggs to raise as our own; they never hatched for some reason. But before I go into details about my own story, I would like to tell you about my roots and some of the influences that have helped make me who I am today. Before there was music or singing, before there was faith, before there was anything that ever mattered to me deeply, there was always my family. They were and are my anchor, my roots, the base of everything that I am and everything that I aspire to be. Without them, my story would be meaningless, because at the end of it all (or at the beginning of it all, I should say), it is family that matters most.

I was born in North Miami, Florida, the second of five kids. We lived in a small one-bedroom apartment in Hialeah, Florida, a city mostly made up of Cubans, which made for a very Latin environment, with lots of salsa and Spanish-language music floating all around our home. Music was always playing in our house: nineties pop music, salsa, jazz, church music, Christmas music, Kansas and seventies rock, and all kinds of different wonderful music that brought a sense of joy and celebration to our everyday lives. Songs and melodies were always a part of our routine, whether it was for fun, for a special occasion or for anything else that might come up. We would always find opportunities to sing together, whether just for family and relatives, caroling to all the neighbors during the holidays or visiting the elderly. It was a way that we felt we could share our love for family, God and others. To us, music and spirituality always went hand in hand in our home, and our family was largely shaped by the way we would combine the two.

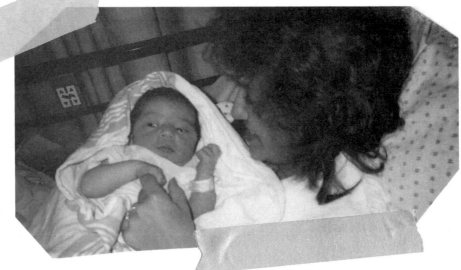

The first time I ever met my mom

Courtesy of the author

My parents say that I started walking when I was seven months old. I also supposedly started speaking more in Spanish than English at first. I know I spent a lot of time with my grandma, my *abuelita*, and I remember the comforting smell of homemade chicken soup simmering in the kitchen, or fresh homemade flour tortillas being grilled for one of our many family get-togethers—the scents mingling with sounds and rhythms of all kinds of pop, dance, salsa or classic jazz. It's fun to think about this stuff again now, because for the last few years all I've ever been asked about was my "music past." It's nice to try to remember what it was like before everything changed.

Like I said, I believe family is so important, especially in Latin culture. When we lived in Florida, my cousins were the center of my universe. My sister Claudia and our cousins were essentially my social life. Without family, we feel empty. They're the ones who carry you, support you, raise you and love you unconditionally. To me, family is the center of everything. The people on both sides of my family have been really important in my life. They've taught me so much about what matters in life and they've been my strength throughout mine. I wouldn't have been able to accomplish anything without them. So let me tell you about my family.

My mom, Lupe, was born in San Pedro Sula, Honduras, the youngest of four close-knit sisters, who, like us, loved singing and dancing and would put on all kinds of local shows and performances when they were little kids. She's really beautiful, my mom. She's looked the same my whole life. She doesn't age. Maybe it was all the salsa and merengue, basketball and singing. She's had six kids (one, a little brother, was stillborn), and she still looks like she's twenty-five. My mother wasn't known only for her great personality, but also for her beautiful singing voice, which everyone always says has a beautiful, full sound and tone and a natural sense of expression. She was usually the lead vocal in all the shows she would do with her sisters, and her own mother, my grandma, always had the dream of her youngest daughter becoming a famous singer like Selena or Gloria Estefan. My mother and aunts got plenty of local exposure because in addition to being wonderful performers, they were also skilled basketball players in a town where high school athletics were part of the community's culture, morale and everyday life. My mom played on the national basketball team and was regularly written about in the local press. My grandfather, her father, was a well-respected journalist in his own right who was known for writing editorials for the town paper. The whole family was well known and liked by the La Ceiba community. But they were extremely poor. My grandparents had always wanted more opportunities for their daughters than what they had growing up in La Ceiba.

When my mom was twelve, her sisters and mom all met some missionaries from the Church of Jesus Christ of Latter Day Saints, which changed their lives forever. It soon became the center of their lives and they devoted their time to helping the missionaries share their message. When my mother was fourteen, the family decided to move to the United States, where they could participate more actively in their new church and hopefully have more opportunities than they could find in their beloved Honduras. My grandparents also hoped the girls would have more prospects in the United States to meet the right kinds of guys. The family arrived in Florida with big hopes to continue working on their musical goals, especially for my mom, whom they all believed showed real promise as a performer. My grandma would take her youngest daughter to various small venues in Miami, where she would sing and dance in front of crowds that seemed to love her. The small local audiences would respond really well, and some also expressed interest in producing and possibly managing her. My mom and grandma even moved to New York for a while to see if they could figure out what to do with my mother's talents, but nothing really materialized and they soon returned to Miami. A short time later, my mom would meet my dad, and after a four-month courtship, they were married. Over the next ten years, four of my siblings and I would later be born.

Courtesy of the author

The Archuleta kids: Claudia, Daniel, Jazzy, Amber and myself

I was always especially close with my older sister, Claudia, probably because we were only about fifteen months apart and always looked like we were about the same age. We were so imaginative back then, and sometimes I wish I could still access those parts of my creativity today. My younger brother, Daniel, and I were quite opposites. When he was really young, we would have him play different parts in the games or whatever we were playing. He had a LOT of energy and loved to play team sports like baseball and football. I tried T-ball but was more interested in the feeling of just being in the outfield in a sunny day than in who was actually winning. Being so outgoing, Daniel had a lot of friends and spent most of his time with them, and he loved playing team sports like baseball and football, which were never really my thing. I've always loved my brother, and although he was Mr. Jock on the outside, he has a very sensitive heart on the inside. He's also become quite a talented singer/songwriter—all self-taught. As a matter of fact, we didn't even know that he was learning to play the guitar by downloading tabs off the Internet. But it wasn't until I was away from home a lot that I really started to realize how much I appreciated him.

If it's true what they say about the apple not falling far from the tree, well, we had two trees that were equally passionate about music, because just like my mom, my dad, Jeff, was also born into a family that was deeply rooted in the magic of sound. On his mother's side, there was my grandma Claudia who had a strong connection to music.

I believe family is so important . . .

It began with her dad, "Gramps," my great-grandpa, who I knew and listened to as he played jazz standards whenever we would go visit him and "Gram." He was a teacher and also at night was a professional jazz piano player in the late forties, fifties and sixties during the "Big Band" era. His style was very much like Erroll Garner and Nat King Cole. He loved to play and listen to what they call "the standards," which were songs that jazz musicians liked to play and improvise over the chord progressions of the many wonderful songs of that era. So my grandma Claudia and her sisters were all influenced by these songs as well as many of the classic musicals of that period. They would always perform little skits with choreography and singing for special events or during the holidays.

Interestingly, my gramps learned to play the trumpet too and during World War II, he was actually a gunner and "Bugler" on his battleship, the USS *Pringle*. As they were traveling toward Okinawa, they were attacked by a Japanese kamikaze plane, and his adored trumpet sank with the ship! The story goes that he was forced to swim to safety through shark-infested waters and literally had to fight off sharks as he swam. I know he received two Purple Hearts for his courage. When

CHORDS OF STRENGTH

he returned, he never played the trumpet again, but he continued to play piano professionally to support his family and so music became a cornerstone of their lives.

Anyway, my grandma Claudia was the oldest of her siblings and by far the most musical. That meant she was in charge of the performances that she and her sisters would perform and she loved to choreograph, sing and perform from a very young age. She developed a real passion for music as well as an amazing performance and acting talent. I'm told she had an amazing, powerful singing voice and that she was an accomplished musical theater actress. She performed regularly in musicals, plays and even did commercials, other television gigs, and acted in a few movies. She had the lead role in several theater productions and was well known throughout Salt Lake City as the "little lady with the big voice." Anytime a film production would come through Utah, she was guaranteed to have some small part. She knew every song by Barbra Streisand, Frank Sinatra, and Bing Crosby who were a few of her favorites. She also performed songs from the movies and musicals of her time like *Singin' in the Rain*, *Funny Girl*, *White Christmas*, *The Music Man*, *The Pajama Game*, and *A Chorus Line*, to name a few. She carried on her tradition with my dad and his sisters, and every year during the holidays they would develop musical numbers that the family would all perform, a tradition we continue to this day.

My dad's father, James Archuleta, also loved music and sang and performed in a barbershop quartet, which is a really difficult skill because you have to be able to harmonize and your pitch has to be just about perfect. In a barbershop quartet, it's not only about being up there and singing on your own, but also about knowing how to make beautiful music as part of a group.

Because of my grandma's involvement in the theater, it was no surprise that my dad got into musical theater as a child. My grandma and my dad were actually both in a professional production of *The Music Man*. My grandma was one of the "pick a little, talk a little ladies" and my dad played one of the main roles, the little boy Winthrop, when he was only eleven years old. My dad grew up appearing in other plays too, and as hard as it is for me and my siblings to believe, he tells us that he really enjoyed singing when he was young. He sang and played piano but then, like his grandpa, he discovered the trumpet! I still have a hard time believing that my dad enjoyed singing because all I had really grown up knowing him to be is a jazz trumpet player. We always had a hard time getting him to sing with us, but he would sometimes, reluctantly.

So my grandma Claudia was twenty when my dad was born and my great-grandma Violet Diehl was only twenty when his mom was born. Since they were both so young, and my dad was the first grandson, he was able to spend a lot of time around his mom's siblings and grandparents who exposed him to a wide range of music from both generations. This is probably why he had an unusually broad understanding of music for someone his age. My dad grew up in the sixties and seventies, but he had influence from the fifties when jazz music was "pop" music. As he became older, he listened to his dad's records of the Kingston Trio, Peter, Paul and Mary, the Everly Brothers, and most important, a few albums from various groups that changed his whole concept of music, *Meet the Beatles*, Dave Brubeck's *Time Out*, and Herb Alpert and the Tijuana Brass. He never looked back and ended up minoring in music in college and playing trumpet with some great bands after graduating. His broad music influences and love and appreciation of music are a big part of who he is today. It's fun to see how it has literally been passed from generation to generation, and to understand and see how much it has come to influence me. If he had not loved musicals, he would never have recorded that PBS special one night of the tenth anniversary of *Les Misérables*, and I may not have ever realized how much music would mean to me. I grew up singing songs from musicals, great R & B classics, and many classic pop songs, and my dad often arranged the music just enough to make it different or more special. His influence on me, and the lessons I've learned from him about music, are definitely reflected through my own approach to singing.

After college, he began hosting clinics to teach kids the concepts of improvisation in music, helping them understand how to take a melody and make it their own. He has taught me to think about those same things ever since I was young: the concept of building little surprises and moments into a song, and how important it is to change it up a bit so that it doesn't always sound the way people are used to hearing it.

During the time we were in Miami he was able to perform with some of the giants of Latin jazz and had the privilege of playing among many world-class, legendary musicians, such as Arturo Sandoval.

Courtesy of the author

My mom, my dad, Claudia, and me

When my parents starting dating seriously, they used to go dancing almost every night at a different club or hotel mostly around Miami Beach. Once they were married and a few years later when Claudia and I were very young, we lived for a time with my grandma and her husband "Angel" for a while at her *finca*, which is the Spanish word for "farm" or "ranch." They raised chickens, and my sister and I used to love to go there and play with them. I spent time out back watching the chickens and the new baby chicks for hours on end. When I was about three, we moved from Hialeah to Hollywood—yes, there is a Hollywood, Florida—between Miami and Fort Lauderdale. We moved into a three-bedroom townhome, the first home that our family actually owned. There were ten townhomes in our development, and my sister and I really enjoyed talking to our neighbors and spending time out by the duck pond in the backyard looking for duck eggs. The weather was always humid in the summer months so we spent a lot of time outside playing with the ducks and catching frogs and lizards and tadpoles that we'd find swimming around in the pond. The ducks would always come follow us looking for food, and my mom would give us bread to break into little pieces to feed them. We were happy there and thought it was so wonderful to have such a big house after living in the little one-bedroom apartment we had lived in before. This house had three bedrooms, and to us, it was gigantic! We even had a downstairs and upstairs and a separate room that became our playroom, where we started playing "Dinosaur Land," which was basically the two of us assembling all our toys (most of which were dinosaur themed) in our own little made-up universe where anything could happen. And, oh boy, everything did happen—flying dinosaurs, and not just pterodactyls, in our Dinosaur Land. Whenever we got a new toy, we would find a way to make it part of Dinosaur Land. That's about the time my little brother was born. Not Daniel, but the one who was stillborn. My mom went to the hospital to have a baby when I was about two years old and had a full term pregnancy that ended with a stillborn baby boy who looked perfect. It was sad, but our religious beliefs really helped our family to get through it, because we know we'll get to see him and know him sometime in the future. But sometimes, I can't help but wonder about him. I wonder if he likes to sing. He would have been in between Daniel and me so maybe he'd have bridged that gap of interests between the both of us. Maybe he'd like sports more than me and like duck safaris better than Daniel.

Later, when we moved to Utah, my dad helped form a salsa band

and he thought it would be great to have my mom as the vocalist and front person with him on trumpet. I remember my mom reminding me of a cross between Gloria Estefan and Selena. I don't know how it can be that I can't dance!

Given our family's love of music, my mom always treated our opportunities to perform seriously, working on teaching us harmonies to the songs and original choreography for each occasion. She would organize family talent shows including our cousins with different configurations of kids, and every holiday there would be a fun-filled variety show for all the relatives to enjoy. I remember at every Christmas, we'd dress up in playful Santa caps and learn carols in three-part harmony. Then we would go to all our neighbors and sing a few songs to them. My mom was such a whiz at coordinating these performances, and we happily went along with her because it was completely normal for us— it's just how we grew up. Our mini-shows entailed more than just casually singing songs around the house; we took them very seriously, and everyone was enthusiastic and eager to participate. When we lived in Florida, we were able to get a piano in our house when I was about four years old. My mom wasn't really a trained piano player, but she did know a few songs and the ones she knew, she played really well. My mom taught me how to play a few familiar Christmas songs including "The Little Drummer Boy." When I started, I had a really hard time playing it with my hands so small. But I really liked the jumps in my right hand. I used to practice those chords at the beginning until I felt I had it just right!

my mom always treated our opportunities to perform seriously

Sometimes I'd sit there and peck out my own melodies. My dad tells me that one time, he asked me what I was playing and I was like "Oh, this is about my dreams." It was like a chase scene in a movie, and a few days later, my dad said he heard me playing it again. I guess I was composing music without realizing what I was doing at the time.

In Florida, I started kindergarten at Pasadena Lakes Elementary when I was five. My teacher was Ms. Cruz; the kids called her Ms. Cruel because sometimes she seemed really mean. After living in Hollywood for a few years, my dad had this feeling that we needed to move out of South Florida, so soon after my sister Jazzy was born, we moved up to Deltona, which is in Central Florida about halfway between Orlando and Daytona Beach. I was almost six and was excited about the new adventure, moving to another new house with more space. My mom's sister Miriam and her family lived there, and they had kids about the same age as us, so we were excited to go up there and had instant friends to play with.

I started going to a new school, Friendship Elementary, and have some great memories even though I only attended there for few months. Come on, who wouldn't be happy at a school named "Friendship"? Just puts a smile on your face.

Our family moved around quite a bit in our early years as my dad was trying to figure out what kind of work would allow him to best take care of our family. Soon after we moved to Deltona, he came across a really great opportunity to work in Utah with one of his old friends, where he'd been longing to return to for years. He never really felt at home in Florida, and deep down he knew that we belonged in Utah and that this was the chance he finally had to get us all there. My mom didn't want to leave her family, but she agreed that it would be a good opportunity for us, so off we went. We had a garage sale and sold practically all of what we had including our second car and all of our furniture and most of our toys and bikes, and packed up the family van with our stereo equipment and speakers. We had it transported to Utah and the remaining items we owned, all packed into fourteen boxes, were sent by truck, and all of the family flew from Orlando to Utah. My dad found a house for us to rent in Murray, and we moved into a wonderful neighborhood, the same one we moved back into several years later and where our family lives today.

As our new Murray neighbors found out our family was musically inclined, we got asked every now and then to perform at a few church activities and weddings and even some funerals. One early memory I have is when my mom had Claudia and me learn a fun dance to a traditional Spanish folk song by Gloria Estefan. She got us some white clothes, and I had a straw hat and bandanna, and we did an authentic dance and learned some choreography that my mom taught us. We performed it at a few places, and at that point, I just danced but didn't really sing by myself in front of people. For church events, we would sing popular songs and harmonize together, and sometimes we were also invited to perform at hospitals and nursing homes for the elderly and sick.

When we first arrived in Utah, my mom, who still really wanted to develop her own skill as a singer, started taking vocal lessons with a girl in our neighborhood. One Saturday, she told us she was going to a seminar being hosted by another vocal teacher in town, Brett Manning. One of Brett's keynote speakers was going to be the legendary Seth Riggs, famous for working with people like Natalie Cole, Michael Bolton, Ray Charles, and Stevie Wonder, just to name a few. In fact, Riggs was the only vocal coach that Michael Jackson ever worked with. My mom ended up taking classes with Brett, and with just a few lessons, she improved dramatically. She would practice by singing mostly pop songs, including Spanish pop songs by Selena and Gloria Estefan and "On My Own" from *Les Misérables*.

Within about six months of moving into Murray, we outgrew the house and had to move to another house in Murray because my dad's new business of buying and selling computer equipment kept needing more room to store everything. We stayed there for another six months and then moved to a really nice house, in Centerville. We found a family who was going to be gone on a church mission for two years and who wanted a family to rent their home while they were gone. It was not your typical house. We called it "the mansion" because it was humongous, and we had several acres as our yard to play in! The youngest member of our family, my little sister Amber, was born while we lived there. I also remember that our neighbors had a pot-bellied pig who always seemed to be out laying down in their front yard, or at least that's what we would always see whenever we passed by their house. I was really into video games as a little kid—like Zelda and all the Nintendo 64 games; and I was fanatical about the Pokémon games, too. I could easily spend hours on these types of activities. Up until I was about thirteen, I was also obsessive about science and anything that had to do with the natural world, which probably explains my interest in ducklings and baby chickens.

I loved watching the National Geographic channel. I was fascinated with dinosaurs and wanted to know everything about them. I was definitely a bit of nerd back then—heck, I still am. I loved cryptozoology, like Bigfoot and Chupacabra and the Loch Ness Monster. The less the possibility something could be real, the more I liked it. I'd waste afternoons absorbed in musty books about those legends as well as astronomy, geology and marine biology (aren't giant squids so freaky?) in the public library. Nature is really amazing. How do some of these things even exist? It gives me goose bumps sometimes, when I really think about it. Haven't you ever looked out the window on a pretty day and wondered how it's possible anything could be so beautiful?

I also had two cats—Midnight and Cloudy—and they were pretty awesome, as far as cats go. They kept me company most of the time. I never wanted to separate from them, and hung out with them any chance I could get. They weren't just regular cats; they would play tag with me and cuddle, so whenever I felt lonely, they were right there to make me feel better. I really enjoyed them. Until they both got pregnant. Twice each. After the first time, whenever it was their time of the month, I used to stay up late to try to chase away this big tomcat who would howl when he would come over to court my cats. I fell asleep frequently trying to discourage him from staying around, and sometimes I would outlast the tomcat, and sometimes I wouldn't. My dad would find me crashed on the sofa and carry me up to my room. That tomcat ended up fathering over ten kittens. Needless to say, I didn't have the cats for very long after that. Plus, we were ready to move to a new house where we really couldn't have any pets so we had to give them away, which was sad, but I knew we had to do it.

And in between my hanging out in libraries and on the couch watching nature shows or tending to my cats, I'd go out and rollerblade, which is just an awesome way to get to know your neighbors. If there was someone I didn't know, I would just stop and say hi. I loved moving fast, gliding around from place to place and taking in all the local scenery while I was at it. I looked forward to waking up the next morning and feeling my sore muscles from the day before. It always felt gratifying to know that I had worked hard enough to get sore. When I'd go alone, it almost felt like I had the world to myself—because I kept moving and no one could catch me.

I could stop and be social, which I really enjoyed, especially helping some neighbors who would be out working in their gardens. Sometimes I would stop to help them and they would try to give me money but I wouldn't ever take it because I just wanted to be nice to them without expecting to be paid.

One time, a neighbor wouldn't let me say no and I went home and showed the money to my parents and said I didn't really want it but she insisted. I kind of felt bad about it but I didn't really know what else I could do. Rollerblading and just walking around the neighborhood was something that allowed me to have a lot of special memories. Riding around on those blades felt like total freedom.

Something else that was important to me was that although my life was changing because of music, some things didn't change. In my church, the scouting program is part of what we do from the time we are eight until we reach the age of eighteen. We start off as Cub Scouts, at twelve become Boy Scouts, and the crowning achievement of that program is to get your Eagle Scout award. I never really thought that I was cut out for scouts; I wasn't really into camping and winter overnight trips and boating and doing the things that you usually did for scouts. I imagined that it was meant more for the kids that were into sports and hunting and fishing. I just didn't think that I was the Eagle Scout type. Maybe I just wasn't motivated enough. Not outdoorsy enough. Plus, to get your Eagle, you need to show leadership skills. I just never really saw myself as enough of a leader. I was just David, who could maybe lead his dog across the street. On a leash.

But my church leaders believed in me and especially one of our neighbors, Cal Madsen. They all kept asking me if I needed help and even taught me how to tie knots, how to pitch a tent, how to prepare for emergencies, how to be a good citizen, and lots of other neat skills that might come in handy some day. Cal made sure I had all the required merit badges and then helped me with the necessary steps to progress through the various ranks of Star, then Life, and ultimately Eagle. Scouting didn't come naturally for me, but with some encouragement and persistent prodding, I was actually doing it. I was getting a bunch of merit badges and actually enjoying getting them. Too bad it all got cut short when I started *American Idol*.

HIT WITH INSPIRATION

"If you can dream it, you can do it"

—WALT DISNEY

It's cool how an artist comes up with an idea that influences another artist and it keeps changing and moving from one person to the next; creativity has a way of recycling and reinventing itself with the passage of time. It's almost as if each artist contributes something unique to a massive bank of ideas and expressions that's accessible to everyone, which future artists later have the privilege of tapping into when it's time for their own creations to come about. So, if creativity is a force that's passed down from artist to artist and generation to generation, then I like to believe inspiration is the thread that ties it all together. Inspiration is fluid; it can move from one person to another at any given moment,

Looks like I was deep in thought in this one . . . or just really into that 3D film!

through any given manner. To me, the feeling of being inspired is what happens when something strikes you so intensely that it triggers something deep inside and sparks your creativity to do something you haven't done before. And then depending on how you choose to respond, it can allow you to be an inspiration to someone else in turn. In any kind of art, inspiration is contagious. The way I see it, without inspiration, we're all like a box of matches that will never be lit.

My dad took me to a high school track one evening the summer after we'd moved to Utah. He was scoping it out for exercise, admiring how new and fresh it looked. He brought all of us kids along. I was just six at the time, but I thought it looked pretty cool too, so I started running around it, for fun, my little feet pounding the pavement. I ran a lap and my dad was impressed and yelled out to me, "Great job, David. Ready to go?"

No, I wasn't. I didn't tell him that, though. I didn't answer him at all. I just kept running. And running. You know, like in the movie *Forrest Gump*? This is what my family must have felt, wondering when I was going to quit running. I ran three miles that night but I could have kept going. I guess when I decide I like something, I can't get enough of it. That kind of singular focus sums me up pretty well, actually. And not just when it comes to running.

When we had just moved to Utah, I remember being downstairs with my brother Daniel playing while my mom was upstairs unpacking and my dad was getting ready to go do some computer work. Before he left, he realized that we were probably going to run out of things to do and wanted to make sure we had something to keep us busy. He had recorded the *Les Misérables* tenth anniversary concert when we were still in Florida and put the VCR on so we could watch it to at least keep us occupied for a little while. So there we were among the zipping open of taped-up cardboard boxes and the popping and snapping of plastic packing material, when I heard something that would change me forever. The first song, "Look Down," was a fun song that Daniel and I both acted out with the other "prisoners" on the TV screen. We quickly learned that song and proceeded to learn all the rest within just a few hours. There was one song, "Castle on a Cloud," sung by the character, Cosette, the young daughter of one of the show's female protagonists. The melody was sad and beautiful in that haunting sort of way, and for some reason, I decided to think that was the best song for me to learn because I was about the same age as her. I just couldn't get enough of *Les Miz*, including all the accents and even the racy song "Lovely Ladies" (which I had no idea what it was about, I promise). Though I couldn't possibly understand then what all the songs were about, I understood very clearly that it had struck me deep in the heart. My eyes were fixed on these performers, and that music captivated me that afternoon and for many years to come. I had never felt so much passion for anything like that before. Until then, all I had known about music was salsa and jazz from my parents, Christmas songs, and a few children's videos we really enjoyed like Silly Songs, Wee Sing, and I hate to admit it, some Barney songs, as well as some primary songs that we would sing at church. The quality of these Broadway songs had a totally new and different effect on me; it was a subconscious reaction that made me want more.

The first day my dad gave us the video, he was gone all day, I think for about twelve hours. When he came home, guess where we were? Still in front of the video, with about half of the songs memorized already. I'd literally beg my parents to play the video over and over again for us, which they did, despite being somewhat surprised by our sudden interest in what usually is considered a more adult musical. Each time we would press play, Daniel would wait for his part, Gavroche, and I would wait for "my parts"—both the male and female. It didn't matter, we took turns singing each song, and quickly had them memorized word for word. I definitely didn't even understand the plot of the show. I mean, really, I didn't even know what a plot was at that time. It didn't matter, as I wasn't driven by the story but instead by the emotion that filled the room each time I'd hear that beautiful music. The melodies were magical to me, mysteriously warming me from the inside every time I would hear them. Something about it just consumed me. I would even try to mimic the accents as closely as I could, which I guess was my way of further connecting to the magic that I was feeling for myself. It was an unconscious pull toward something that I couldn't possibly understand in any intellectual way—but something that I knew I was totally obsessed with. Singing seemed to fill a void I didn't know I had, and from this point on, I was completely hooked.

Since we didn't have a piano when we moved to Utah, my dad got my sister and me one of those Casio electronic keyboards that came with one hundred and one different songs with lighted keys. We would try to learn these simple little songs and would take turns playing them for each other. We never paid attention to what was playing on the radio; we preferred making our own music or listening to our favorite musicals. Besides *Les Misérables*, we also loved *Into the Woods, Joseph and the Amazing Technicolor Dreamcoat*, and *Evita*. I even tried out opera for a little while after hearing an opera appreciation computer CD my dad brought home one day. There was one song that played automatically whenever you would put the CD in the drive, and I would sing right along with it. It was a song for high sopranos so I had my work cut out for me, but I remember enjoying it immensely until I moved on to my next phase of musical discovery.

Meanwhile, while my parents were performing with their salsa band, they also were able to perform at a Mexican restaurant, Garcia's, up in Layton. It was just the two of them and a guitar player friend, Kenji. My dad played the flügelhorn while my mom sang and Kenji would accompany my mom, then play something with my dad. They would do songs with karaoke tracks and trio arrangements, and one day, they told me if I would come and sing, I could have anything free I wanted off the menu, which was a special treat for me and made it an offer I couldn't refuse. I willingly accepted the invitation to perform and poured my heart out singing my rendition of "Castle on a Cloud" and songs from *Evita*. At the time, I honestly didn't think anyone was paying any attention to me, but there was this waitress who put a tip in the little cup that sat at the foot of the stage, and I remember seeing her face while I sang this particular song and thought she

Claudia and me, always two peas in a pod

was just feeling sorry for me and trying to make me feel good because I was a little kid.

The next summer, when I was nine years old, my dad surprised my sister and me with season passes to the famous one-hundred-year-old Lagoon Amusement Park in Farmington, which was close to our town of Centerville, about ten miles north of Salt Lake City. The passes meant that we could visit the park three or four times per week if we wanted to, which of course we did, loving each visit more than the last. Man, that place was awesome. Arcades! Roller coasters! Games! Food! And music!

We were totally ecstatic. After all, the place was overflowing with fun, all kinds of games, and our personal favorite: musical groups that performed all kinds of awesome musical numbers. We really liked the OK Corral Western performers, who would always hang out with us after their performances and make us feel special, and also the group of "zombies" who would sing and perform fun pop songs. One of their signature tunes that summer was Natalie Cole's "Pink Cadillac," which would stay in my mind forever and make her one of my musical role models to this day.

The next school year, we moved from Centerville to Sandy, and I started fourth grade. For Christmas that year, my aunt Char bought me a Natalie Cole greatest hits CD, which I would listen to over and over again, and for a talent show, a girl who I knew from OnStage, Janey, asked if I wanted to sing a duet with her of "Pink Cadillac." I was a little nervous and thought everyone was going to laugh because it was a song that I didn't think they would know, or maybe they would think I sounded like a girl. But my mom helped Janey and me and together took that very song and choreographed our own little skit to perform for the class complete with a cardboard version of a pink Cadillac. We loved all of the soulful R & B licks and, with the kind of determination only ten-year-olds could have, we were going to get everything right, even if it was just for an audience of kids and teachers.

Even at that age, I didn't want to just sound soulful, I wanted to be soulful. I would try to listen and learn from other singers, and I seemed to be drawn to the songs with dramatic moments in them and did my best to try to find where the magic in the music lived. What was it that made it real? What was it that made you feel it so deeply?

My mom had learned a lot about vocal technique when she studied with Brett Manning and she started to help me with my technique, while my dad taught me the basic concepts of how to make a song sound your own. He would say, "David, instead of sounding exactly like the person on the record you hear, why don't you change things up a bit?" I soon began to understand that this could make my singing special. No matter what famous song I would sing, my goal became to give people the impression that they were hearing and experiencing that song for the very first time.

Looking back, I think I learned important concepts about musicianship at a very young age without realizing it. I didn't learn them consciously, but they were definitely coming through. I guess I started internalizing these things when I didn't even know any better, and I have my parents and grandparents to thank for that.

By the time I was ten, a bunch of my relatives were trying to convince my dad that I should go to Hollywood and take my singing to the next level. Fortunately, he was a bit more realistic and assured our well-intentioned relatives that when the time was right, we would think about doing something and that there was still plenty of time and no hurry. How many ten-year-olds have had music careers? OK, maybe Michael Jackson and Billy Gilman or maybe even Donny Osmond, but I didn't really know anything other than that I loved to sing and was passionate about it. My dad knew a little bit about how things work in the music business, and he didn't want to overreact or jump the gun. But more than that, I think both my parents just wanted me to have a healthy and normal childhood. My dad always used to say there's a difference between being "good for Utah" and being "good overall."

Things will happen when they are supposed to and he didn't want us to get ahead of ourselves.

He wasn't wrong to be this cautious, because the truth is that in those days, even though I loved singing and was starting to do so more regularly, I was still pretty uncomfortable with the sound of my own voice. When I sang, it was usually in the playroom with the door closed. My dad would hear me singing full out, and because I was too busy belting it out, I usually didn't hear him approach. But he'd tap on the door and say encouraging words such as "David, will you open the door for a minute? I just want to tell you you're doing a great job! Your vibrato is sounding awesome!" or "Your intonation sounds great!" or "You are using dynamics really well, do you know what that means?" or "The way you are singing is very impressive for being so young!" He said I wasn't just singing the song but that I was also instinctively conveying emotional ideas. I had a sense that I knew what he was talking about but that didn't change the fact that I still hated the way I sounded.

So I'd stop singing. Of course.

I guess I was okay singing with the relatives and even for the occasional show with my parents; but mostly, I still didn't understand how people other than my family could want to hear me sing. I'd be pretty nervous; I didn't think I was good at all and I'd anticipate for someone to tell me to stop singing or boo me off the stage. But nobody ever did.

Though our dad was always there to help me with my music, I was also very close to my mom and her side of the family, especially because we grew up in Florida and were with our cousins and relatives from her side almost constantly. Also, because we moved around quite a bit, there were periods of time when our mom felt that it was best for us to be home schooled, which she did on and off for four or five years. She spent hours at the library and online to find creative ways of teaching us math and spelling and always encouraged us to read a lot. She was already teaching us before we got to kindergarten and chose to continue with home school between schools and when we were moving around figuring out what we were going to do as a family. She felt that we were just fine at the age we were at doing both public school and home school and felt strongly that it would give us the rare chance to spend as much time with one another as possible, which I think was more of a benefit than the actual learning.

Spending all that time with my mom meant also learning through her musical talents. I'd always try to mimic her. Whenever I heard her do a certain song, it would become my personal goal to figure out how to do it myself. Even though I didn't like the way I sounded, it never stopped me from trying to get it right. As I saw it then, each song was an opportunity to get better and better, no matter who was listening.

Courtesy of the author

My mom,
Claudia, and I
having a laugh

I remember at one point, she was really into Christina Aguilera's song *"Contigo en la Distancia,"* which has all kinds of complicated runs and licks, the kind of song that's usually sung by mature female R & B singers (or Christina Aguilera). My parents would encourage my attempts to nail the song, and amused by my ambitiousness, they were curious to see how far I'd be able to take it. I took this reaction as a challenge, as it just made me want to learn and perfect the song even more. My dad noticed that it seemed like it was easier for me to listen and mimic the phrasings that Christina Aguilera was doing than it was for my mom, and he kept telling me I was sounding better and better. Maybe it was that natural sense you have as a kid: that you had the energy and determination to want to prevail against the odds. I told myself that I would learn that song, which was the start of my understanding that I could actually control the sound of my voice.

About that same time, my parents felt that it might be the appropriate time to start looking for opportunities and explore what was out there for a kid like me. As it turned out, my mom happened to come across a flyer for the 2001 Utah talent competition. Intrigued at the idea, she signed me up for the junior division—without asking me first. Of course, when I found out about the upcoming show, I was really upset and resented the fact that she had done this without my consent. I was barely able to sing for the few folks at the restaurant without my cheeks turning beet red, so I couldn't imagine the possibility of singing for a huge crowd of people who were actually expecting to see real talent. This wasn't just a performance, it was a "talent competition," which scared me to death. I didn't feel that I had it in me to compete.

At first I didn't say anything out of respect for my mom, and because I didn't want to be a downer. But I felt a huge conflict. Of course, there was no question that I loved to sing, but you know how your own voice sounds strange when you hear a recording of it? Well, mine was like that, but exponentially more extreme. I just couldn't stand to hear my voice and it honestly really bothered me. So the thought of singing in a talent competition would be a whole new dimension for me, and weeks before the show was even slated to take place, I already felt that I was way out of my league.

My parents, who I believe saw the local talent show as a great opportunity for me to grow personally, sat me down and gave me an honest, motivating speech that I still hold close today. It was one of those talks that I remember vividly, the kind that shape you as a kid, and in my case, as a singer. They were by no means trying to push or pressure me into doing anything that I didn't want to, and instead were trying to help me see that just maybe I would share some joy with others through this opportunity if I would be willing to share my talent with them. They gently told me that this show would be a perfect chance for me to make other people feel good, which, as they explained, is what talent is meant for. They reminded me that my gift was not something to keep to myself, and that in fact, "even the Bible teaches us that we are not supposed to hide our light under a bushel; that we are instead supposed to let our light shine bright." They tried to help me realize that when I sang, it made people feel something special, and that the simple act of singing allowed me to contribute something positive to the world. They basically stripped it down for me by telling me that I was blessed with a gift from God and that it could be a really nice thing to share this gift with the world. Although now I appreciate everything they told me, at the time, I didn't see it that way. I remember thinking that my parents just wanted to show me off, and my mom felt terrible for signing me up in the first place.

The day of the show, I was a total wreck. I was not excited about having to do this and was feeling more and more resentment that my mom had done this crazy thing of signing me up and that my dad was going along with her. By this point, my mom felt entirely responsible for the emotional state I was in and didn't want to push me to do the show and was so upset about it that she decided to not even go to the show. My dad, on the other hand, patiently tried to get me to understand that he believed it could be really good for me not just as a singer but for my own personal development as a person. Looking back now, I don't think he was wrong. He sat me down and after trying to persuade me unsuccessfully, very calmly said, "David, do you realize that your name is already in the program? Everybody is counting on you. What's going to happen when they call your name and you don't show up? You know what I think, son? I think the show just won't be the same without you." Well, I guess that did it. In that moment, I understood that I had an obligation to be there and surely I didn't want to be known for letting a bunch of people down. So I went. I was scheduled to be the second child performer, and by the time the show got under way, I was such a nervous, slobbering mess that I could barely get a sentence out. I simply couldn't handle the emotional state of affairs, so it was just my dad and me backstage with the show's coordinators, who by now were also concerned about me.

Granted, I was only ten, but I was having a bona fide panic attack. I felt like my throat was closing up and I was sure I wouldn't be able to sing even one note. My poor dad had no idea what to do. He told me that the choice to go on or not was totally mine, and at this point he really didn't want to see me suffer for another second. He tried to comfort me by saying, "You don't have to do this. But if you want to give it one last shot, I'll be right here to support you. In fact, I have an idea: Why don't we go say a prayer? I bet that will help us through this." For some reason, that idea calmed me down, and together we went around the corner to an empty hallway, where we together said a prayer. My breathing started to go back to normal, and breath by breath, my attitude slowly started to change. My nose was still stuffy, my eyes were a sad shade of pink, and there were only three minutes left before my name was called. I could feel my heart rate start to go back to normal, and I don't know what happened, but something inside clicked, and I built up the nerve to get myself out there. I guess something deep inside told me I had to come through—not for my parents, but instead for myself—and maybe even for God, who was responsible for this so-called gift to begin with.

There were about thirty participants total, and ten of them were kids like me. The performances included songs, dances, instruments, comedy acts and everything in between. It was a beautiful, first-class affair, which to me, being just a boy, came across as elegant, stylish and totally professional. I remember there was even an emcee in a black tuxedo, and the stage was dressed with perfect lighting and a gorgeous backdrop for a set. There was a live band to accompany some of the singers, a complete panel of local celebrity judges, and several hundred people all dressed up in the audience.

My plan was to sing "I Will Always Love You" by Whitney Houston, which begins kind of quietly, a cappella, without any music. I remember noticing that there was a woman singing the same song in the adult division, and I thought, *This is so embarrassing. She sounds so much better than I will. Should I sing another song?* But despite my second thoughts about the song choice, I nervously came up to the microphone and simply started to sing.

From the moment I began, the audience went completely quiet, and before I knew it, I was in a zone of total peace. I couldn't see any one person out there, just this huge sea of smiles and wide eyes all gazing in my direction. The music finally came in and by then the audience started to respond. They stood up, clapping and cheering, probably shocked at such a big song coming from such a little guy. When I saw the audience's reaction, I felt like I had grown six inches. It was such a surprise to look out at all the people there, all of them wild with applause and whistles. After I finished, the emcee called me to come back onstage. He asked me to sing the highest note of the song again and hold it, and even though I was a little confused, I belted the note out once again and just held it until he lowered his hand and put his arm around me and showed me so much support that all my initial fear and concerns disappeared immediately. Maybe I could enjoy performing after all, and maybe it would take this small lesson in bravery for me to understand this basic fact about myself.

As the whole show was about to wrap up, the judges at the table sat huddling and whispering to one another. They were quiet and serious and everyone—contestants and audience members alike—was on edge with curiosity about the results. I was just happy it was all over, and felt a new sense of satisfaction and confidence in myself for having the courage to step up, but I was not really there to compete, and never in a million years did I expect to win.

So you can imagine how I felt when I heard my name called as the winner of the children's division. I had never won anything before in my life, and after the mini-crisis backstage just moments before, winning just didn't seem like an option. I was given a trophy and also a cash prize of three hundred dollars, but most important, I went home with the feeling of confidence, knowing that it wasn't so bad after all singing in front of people. As we were finishing up with the event people, my dad jokingly asked me if I was still mad at my mom for signing me up. I was still coming down from the thrills of the competition, but gave him a look like I wouldn't go that far, but let myself accept that fact that maybe I wasn't so upset anymore. Not only was I not mad at anyone, but I was also now filled with a sense of joy that would always come when I sang from my heart. I knew that I was able to look my fear straight in the eye and, with a bit of faith and courage, could find a way to overcome. I felt happy, accomplished and completely excited about what might come next.

CHAPTER

SCHOOL OF AMERICAN IDOL

"The obstacles of your past
can become the gateways
that lead to new beginnings."

—RALPH BLUM

3

After the Utah Talent Competition, my parents thought that it might be good for me to have some more opportunities to get over my fear of singing in public. They checked around and found out about a few children's performing groups, which is a big thing here in Utah, as there is a great appreciation for the arts, especially singing, musicianship and dancing. My sister and I enrolled in one of these groups called OnStage, which allowed us to perform with other kids that actually seemed to enjoy performing.

We were split into age groups and taught to perform medleys of songs for local audiences. They also had told us how they traveled to other states and countries and one year said they had even gone to Japan! It all sounded like a lot of fun. We were required to wear all kinds of different costumes and showed up at several public events, including the Fourth of July and Twenty-Fourth of July parades and fireworks. I guess I had some fun learning the songs and steps, but I also had the nagging feeling that I didn't want to just sing part of a song, which is what happened when there were twelve to twenty other kids involved; instead, what I was really after was the chance to sing the whole song by myself so I could really put all the passion I was feeling into it. With a group of other kids, it just wasn't the same. I felt frustrated musically so after a few months of that I felt it was time to prepare for something else.

So after finally deciding that I enjoyed singing and having had a positive experience at the Utah Talent Competition, all my relatives were again saying that I should go to Hollywood to try to take my singing to the next level. My dad still had his reservations. He truly believed I was talented, but he wasn't sure just HOW talented I was. Was I just talented for Utah, or was I talented compared to other kids across the country and how could we really know? We had no idea that things would soon be set in motion that would allow us to have the opportunities to find out the answer to that question once and for all.

A year or so after the Utah Talent Competition, my parents and we kids went out shopping for a new car. We visited several of the local dealerships to test drive the models they were considering, and we were all amazed to see that one of the cars had a built-in backseat multimedia system and that it was picking up the local TV channels as well. How cool was that? But even more exciting to me than the idea of a TV in a car was what was on the TV. As we cruised around the Sandy, Utah streets that evening, while my parents focused on things like engines and safety features, my dad put on this channel which had a brand-new show none of us had ever seen before but we had heard about and were excited to see.

We had seen the commercials and we were curious as to what it would all be about, so we started to watch it while we were driving around. They were showing the first round of singing auditions for the very first season of the show that was to become the biggest show ever, of course, *American Idol*. And from that moment on, it's pretty safe to say that I would never be the same.

There were singers in a competition, like *Star Search*, but this new show was JUST singers, not four different categories. And, it seemed like they weren't just a few ordinary singers; it was as if all of these amazing, talented people had suddenly burst out of the woodwork to fulfill their lifelong desire to sing from the soul—like the show was a massive trigger for millions of people all over the country to step forward with their talents and

He truly believed I was talented

dreams. Though the singers were clearly way more advanced than I was, I could somehow relate to them. I felt that the program was talking (or singing) directly to me.

From the beginning of *Idol*, our family became obsessed with the show. We'd sit and watch it together every time it was on, excitedly following the progress of each participant, eagerly watching every twist and turn. We loved the energy of the show, Ryan Seacrest and Dunkleman with their sarcasm and upbeat charisma, and the judges, too, each with their own personality and style. But more than that, we loved seeing these "regular unknowns" show up and belt out songs like true professionals. It was such a diverse showcase of musical possibilities. We had seen a few other shows like *Star Search*, *Making the Band* and had even heard of the UK show *Pop Idol*, but there was something captivating about this show and with us being raised on singing and music, here was a show that totally glorified and celebrated both. And it wasn't simply a singing competition, but you were able to get to know each contestant and you could feel like you really knew them and wanted to encourage them to do well. Each performance was an exercise in interpretation, which called on different aspects of a singer's creativity. The show made the point that it's not enough to have a good voice—you actually have to know what to do with it. And so many of the singers I was hearing on *American Idol* seemed to know exactly what they were doing. I was totally hooked. Certain singers' performances came across to me as an act of pure heart-to-heart communication, a moment defined by this universal force of *human feeling*—a force that on occasion would hit me directly in the soul and make me feel something so special that I couldn't even put into words.

Because my dad is a computer person, he made sure we had TiVo as soon as it was available for our satellite system. So I was able to watch and rewatch the performances that I loved over and over again. Not only that, I could even watch the specific moments in a song that I liked most, which meant that I could study every detail of that singer's arrangement. I took advantage of this to learn a host of new songs that captivated me, and to see how other singers chose to tackle any given song. After each show, I'd run upstairs as fast as I could to our computer room and look up the songs that I'd heard and the ones I was most impressed with from that night. It was as if the first part of my education was to watch the show itself, and the second part was to research what I had seen and heard. I was not just hearing anymore—I was very much *listening*.

When I carefully think back, it strikes me that a big part of my interest in *American Idol* had to do with the singers' desire—their desire to really feel the music and to communicate this to everyone who was out there listening. Sure, you can enjoy songs that play on the radio, but you don't get the chance to watch the artist perform, you don't get to see the look in their eyes, or the passion in their expression. In a way, you don't really get a complete sense of the emotion and feeling behind the performances. But with *Idol*, the performances come alive in a totally new way, a way that makes them so pure and so incredibly close to the essence of what singing is all about. Also, on the radio the vast majority of what you hear is pop. With *Idol*, the variety of music totally blew me away. I was introduced to so many different styles and genres of singing. It almost felt like Music History 101, being taught by some of the greatest legendary teachers out there. In time, I wouldn't just know a handful of classic songs from famous musicals but also some classic Motown, soul and R & B songs, moving through the genres just as the show's contestants had to do every single week. There was a whole new world of music to explore and with the introduction of *Idol* into our home, the floodgates were now wide-open.

After the audition rounds, the show would narrow the field down to the Top 30 contestants. For the next three shows, ten performers would sing each night and America would vote through the Top 3 each night and there would be a wild card to choose the tenth finalist. So, I couldn't wait to see and hear who finally made it and waited with anticipation to hear each group. The very first night of the live shows, the first singer on deck was a girl named Tamyra Gray. This beautiful girl with an even more beautiful voice came out and sang "And I'm Telling You I'm Not Going" from *Dreamgirls*. Back then, I had never heard of that song or the musical *Dreamgirls*, but when I heard her sing that song, it was kind of like a spiritual moment for me. Tamyra came out onto the stage quietly, giving absolutely no hint of the thunderous, soulful outpour that she was about to hit us with. I don't know how she did it, but she delivered so many different emotions during that performance: passion, rage, love, optimism and commitment—*all in less than two minutes!* Never mind that she had a great voice, which was, of course, a given; but this was so much more than a demonstration of singing technique. It was a full-on display of pure emotional range. I felt it all, and I could tell right off the bat that she did, too, belting the song out like some sort of musical mission. If I had ever felt that singing could be something special, now I was sure of how sacred it could really be. Her delivery of that song affected me like few things had ever done before, and in that instant, I was learning so much about who I wanted to be musically.

After she finished, I went straight to our computer and hunted around for the song. It wasn't as quick and easy to find specific music then as it is today and you really had to dig around to find what you wanted. Thankfully, people were recording stuff right off their television sets and posting little musical clips, so I was able to download those, which allowed me to learn many of the songs that struck me.

With *Idol*, the variety of music totally blew me away.

My dad also came up to help me research "And I'm Telling You I'm Not Going" because, just like me, he thought it was completely amazing. Luckily, we were able to find the original version by Jennifer Holliday and a couple of other live performances of her singing it over the years. We didn't know it had been an R & B hit back in the eighties. So I had a new favorite song and the chance to practice it lots of different ways until I found a way to sing it that felt right for me. I sang the song all the time, morning, noon and night. I'd go in the backyard with my cats and sing to them. I always poured my soul into it, even when I was just swinging on the swing set or just walking around our backyard. I literally started to change the way I sang after *Idol* hit the airwaves, not realizing that I was already starting to sound less like a little kid who was into musicals and way more like these soulful, R & B singers who told entire stories through the emotion and feeling in their songs.

My parents felt that it would be a good idea to capture some of these moments while I was still young, so my dad bought some basic equipment for the computer. This gave us the chance to have a mini-recording studio at home, taking our interest in music to the next level of seriousness. He asked if he could record me singing because he felt that it would be special for us to remember what I sounded like at a young age, knowing that in the next few years my voice would change. He said it was really cool to have recordings of stuff he did when he was a kid and thought that it would be something I would appreciate when I was older if not now. He also pointed out that my style was really starting to develop and by recording me, we'd be able to hear how I was progressing. Though I hated the way I sounded, I understood the point of doing this. Even though I was young, I knew enough to trust my parents when it came to music.

While the excitement of the *American Idol* season continued, my dad, knowing of my obsession with Natalie Cole, found out that she

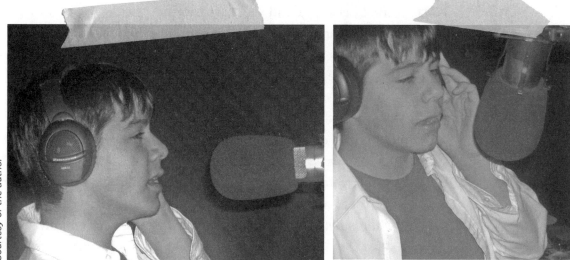

Courtesy of the author

Recording was a great way to monitor my progress and helped me to develop my style.

was scheduled to perform at the prestigious Park City Jazz Festival in Deer Valley, which is about half an hour away from Salt Lake City. He thought it would be fun for us to go hear her perform. We drove to Park City, to the beautiful venue nestled way up in the chilly mountains. I was able to invite a friend with me and although we were probably the youngest people there, I can pretty much guarantee there wasn't anyone there more excited at the chance to hear my current, favorite female vocalist on the planet! Natalie was the final act, and when she came onstage, I was completely and utterly blown away by all of her classic "Unforgettable"-era standards, as well as her older R & B hits, many of which I was hearing for the very first time. She did an encore version of the U2/B. B. King classic, "When Love Comes to Town," which totally blew me away. It felt like such an honor to be in the company of such talent, and to this day, I think it was one of my dad's best-ever ideas.

And the ideas did not stop there. After the show, my dad looked at me and said, "So what do you think about seeing if you could meet Natalie Cole? Let's wait and see if we can meet her." Despite being a little nervous about meeting one of my musical mentors, when he said those words, I was very reluctant. But my dad assured me it would be OK. I think he knew it would be something I would never forget and that could change my life potentially. After much anticipation, Natalie Cole came out and saw us waiting outside her dressing room. It was around midnight; everyone from the audience was gone, and only a few security people were left in the venue milling about.

Despite being totally awestruck, starstruck and freezing, I shyly walked up to her and asked if I could sing her a song. Much to my surprise, she smiled, looked up at my father for a moment and gave us both a yes. I sang my new signature tune "And I'm Telling You I'm Not Going," and I sang it with all my heart! Her beautiful brown eyes lit up while I sang, which was another one of those incredibly special moments that gave me a sense of self-affirmation. *Thank you, Tamyra*

Gray, I thought to myself. *Thanks for the inspiration!* How could anything be more incredible than this?

A week after I sang for Natalie Cole, my dad got a call from an enthusiastic neighbor who happened to be watching the *Jenny Jones Show* and told us that the producers were on the hunt for talented kids. The neighbor asked my dad if she should get more details on our behalf. They agreed, and she called us back a little later with a telephone number for my father to call. He called the show and spoke with a talent producer who said that they were specifically looking for Latino kids with special talents. She explained that the show had many Latin American viewers, so they thought it would be fun to do a show for that demographic. Since my mother was from Honduras and my dad was part Spanish, I was definitely plenty enough Latino that I would fit the bill. "I have an eleven-year-old son who can sing, and I would like to hear what you think about him," my dad said to the producer on the other end of the line. He asked her if she knew the song, "And I'm Telling You I'm Not Going," and offered to play a recording of me singing it over the phone. She said, "The Jennifer Holliday song, of course I know it!" He played the tape and the woman went completely nuts. This was on a Monday. She asked if we could travel to Chicago on Wednesday to appear on the show. My dad was shocked but excited for me and when I heard I had a chance to go to Chicago, we quickly began planning our upcoming unexpected adventure.

On the airplane, my father expressed concern about my ability to stay brave, given my breakdown at the Utah Talent Competition. He didn't want to put undue pressure on me, and he wanted to be sure this experience was a positive one. We decided that I would just go out there and give it my all, and that this experience was meant to be fun. No stress, no expectations—simply fun. I told myself that I would do the best I could and keep reminding myself that enjoying the moment, and being grateful for the opportunity, was the most important thing.

When we arrived in Chicago, we were taken to a really nice hotel near the Sears Tower, which was a total treat for me since I had read about it in *The Guinness Book of World Records*, a book I loved throughout my childhood. Because of how excited I was about this awesome opportunity, it somehow made perfect sense that we were staying near the tallest building in the world. The synergy seemed to crackle magically and everything felt just right.

At the rehearsal, I was up on the stage by myself with the production crew. My father sat in the audience while I prepared for my turn to perform. When it was my turn to rehearse, I just went out there and sang it without any problem. I don't think my dad expected me to deliver the way that I did, which I bet helped to calm his nerves a bit. He later told me that I sang at the rehearsal as if it were the real show, and that he was really proud of me! I think he was shocked because I hadn't really sung publicly in months, and maybe he was worried that I would get cold feet at the last minute. I was just eleven and had no clue who Jenny Jones was, but I was going to be singing on national television for the first time, which fueled me with serious motivation and a need to sing better than I ever had before. When it was time to sing for real, Jenny Jones called me to the stage, and I went out there as if it was what I was always meant to do. I took the microphone with my pudgy little hand and somehow just knew what to do.

When this Chicago audience reacted exactly the same way the Utah audience had—with total delight, applause, smiles and cheers—I felt a special tingling sensation inside and started to believe that this was something I could enjoy doing and that surprisingly, people seemed to really not mind my voice. At that age I couldn't quite articulate what that something might be, but I just felt that I would maybe try this again if I had the chance. It's not that I was already envisioning a future as a singer, but more that I was getting closer and closer to knowing what my true passion might be all about. And there was no question about it: My passion would have a lot to do with music.

During the show, we went to the green room, where, much to my happy surprise, sitting right there was AJ Gil, the *American Idol* contestant who'd made it to the Top 8 that first season. I knew every single song he'd performed on the show and really admired his beautiful tenor voice.

To me, this guy was a huge celebrity and I was completely star struck. Here I was on the *Jenny Jones Show*, sharing a green room with one of the American Idols. This was more than big-time—this was it! I was so overcome with excitement that I couldn't even find the words to talk to AJ. Fortunately, my dad was there to help me out. AJ was so nice and told me that he loved my performance, as well. Not only did I get the privilege of sharing a green room with a singer who I deeply respected, but I had the honor of hearing him say that I was a great singer, too.

nothing was going to stop me from singing my heart out when given the chance.

You probably won't be surprised to hear that when the show aired a few weeks later, I wouldn't even watch it. Every time my parents played it for someone, I would quickly leave the room. My dad actually had to stand in front of the door one time in order to get me to watch it! He felt it was important that I see myself doing something I used to be afraid of. But whether I watched my performance or not had nothing to do with my commitment as a singer. Even though I didn't like the aftermath, nothing was going to stop me from singing my heart out when given the chance.

When we got home from Chicago, our household was bubbling with excitement due to my recent TV appearance. We realized that the next weekend was going to be time for the first *American Idol* finale and my dad had something in mind which would put me in front of more than one of my own favorite Idols, including a trip that would take us to Hollywood.

Shortly after our latest adventure on *Jenny Jones*, my father decided to call his friend Seth Riggs, whom he and my mother had met when she attended the seminar with Brett Manning a few years earlier and for whom my dad had been a computer consultant. He caught Seth up on everything I had done recently, told him that I was really starting to show some promise, and asked if he would be willing to listen to me sing and give us some input on what he thought we should do with me. My parents knew that Seth had worked with a lot of children and they wanted his honest opinion about where I could go from here. Seth was nice enough to agree, and the plan was officially in motion for us to travel to Los Angeles to meet with him.

Now the best part about the rest of this story is that I was clueless as to what my dad was really up to. As far as I knew, all we were doing was going to see Mr. Riggs. What I didn't know was that my father had secretly bought tickets on eBay for us to see the *American Idol* finale live in Los Angeles. I don't think I would have been able to contain myself in the car ride had I known what my dad had up his sleeve. Though he paid upward of two thousand dollars for the tickets, he felt it was justified because it would be a special, once-in-a-lifetime memory for me. We had to drive to Las Vegas to pick up our tickets from the vendor he'd found online. To make friendly conversation, my father casually told the man about my recent *Jenny Jones Show* appearance, and about how passionate we all were about music. Mind you, I still had no idea, but nothing was going to stop me from singing my heart out when given the chance.

I had no idea who this man was or why we were meeting him. When you're a kid, I guess you just blindly assume the adults around you have reasons for what they are doing—I was just happy and grateful to be going on yet another exciting trip. After hearing my dad's stories, the man asked if I would sing for him and his kids. I was still relatively shy but I surprised the group (and maybe even myself) and sang for the mystery man in Las Vegas. I'm sure I would have even taken it up a notch had I known then that he had our tickets to the *American Idol* finale in his jeans pocket.

We continued on to California to Orange County, where my aunt Lauri lives. We spent that first night with her at her house. I was really happy to be in California and to see the ocean and the beaches. When we got there, we heard about a singing contest where you could win tickets to the *American Idol* finale up in Hollywood. It was to take place the following day at the Hollywood & Highland Center, home to the famous Kodak Theatre, the Hollywood Walk of Fame, and the Grauman's Chinese Theatre. It just so happened to also be where the *Idol* finale was!

We knew we had to give it a try. After all, the reason for our trip was all about singing, we were there to meet and take my very first singing lesson from the infamous Seth Riggs (at least that's what I thought the whole reason was at the time)! He lived just a few minutes away from the Hollywood & Highland Center so it seemed like the perfect plan. The three of us would go meet with Seth first and then head up to the contest and see what it was all about. When we walked into the studio to meet Seth, it was quite intimidating, and a bit scary really because I was particularly shy at the age of eleven. At the meeting and lesson with Seth, he was really positive and helpful. He asked me to sing and also had me making some pretty interesting sounds, which I later learned were considered a part of real voice training. So, mission accomplished, we thought. We were now confident and ready to hit the singing contest later that day.

When we arrived, the outdoor venue was totally packed, crawling with eager singers, most of them way older than me. There was definitely something special in the air that day, and it was by far one of the most exciting things I'd ever seen (and this was just the registration)! Everything felt so overwhelming and fast-paced that I didn't even have time to think about how nervous I really was. We waited eagerly in line for what seemed like an hour just to fill out the enrollment forms. And to our surprise, when we finally arrived at the front of the line, we were told , "We are sorry. Our minimum age requirement is sixteen."

So I guess it's true what they say about everything happening for a reason. While we were in line, my aunt walked up with a girl whom she befriended (my aunt does that a lot) named Diane Gordon. She told us that she was a background singer who had toured with Celine Dion, Jessica Simpson and Christina Aguilera. She had also been on Ed McMahon's *Star Search* a few years earlier. Needless to say, we were all very impressed, and though I wouldn't be able to compete because of my age, we at least knew that we were going to have a fun time watching the contest and hanging out with our new friend who was in fact a real professional singer!

It was really fun to hear the different contestants sing and to hear which songs they chose. It was also really fun just looking around at all the different people in Hollywood—to just people watch! After all, Los Angeles is very different from what I was used to seeing in Salt Lake. As the contest was coming to the end and the judges were determining who the winner was going to be, something really remarkable happened. As I was looking around the crowd, I noticed that right there in front of me, just about ten feet away, was none other than several of the *American Idol* finalists themselves! They were just casually hanging around in their sweat suits and sneakers, kind of behind the outdoor stage area, giggling and talking and signing autographs every now and again. Man, I thought, first AJ in Chicago, now more finalists in L.A.? What strange magic could possibly be at work? Was I dreaming? How could all these amazing things be happening at the same time, and how could they possibly be happening to me?

My aunt, always a social butterfly, coaxed me into coming along with her to that part of the stage to say hello. She wasted no time in telling them about my recent appearance on the *Jenny Jones Show* and that it was there that I had met their fellow Idol, AJ Gil. Nikki McKibbin, who came in third that season, was super-nice to us and chatted a bit. She then motioned for my aunt to come close enough for her to whisper something in my aunt's ear. I didn't know what it could possibly be but I was very excited to find out just what this secret was! She had whispered that they were all (including AJ) staying at the Renaissance Hotel right next door. And then, she told my aunt not to tell anyone, and that if we wanted to come by tomorrow morning around nine a.m., we would most likely get a chance to say hello to AJ and maybe even meet Tamyra and Kelly! I couldn't believe it!

As you can probably imagine, that night I couldn't sleep much from all the excitement. It felt like I was part of some kind of lucky dream— and you have to remember that I still didn't know about my dad's incredible surprise. I just thought the whole thing was one massive coincidence; I was simply grateful to be in Los Angeles, and to be able to have even a tiny glimpse into this world of music that I felt so connected to.

The next morning we pulled into the circle in front of the Renaissance Hotel and I looked over and saw Jim and Nikki outside. I looked over at her, not able to say a word. My dad signaled for her to come over to our car and she held up her hand indicating she would be right back. Within a minute or two, there was AJ, just as Nikki had said he would be, and there was I, completely stunned and blown away by this dream of the last twenty-four hours. AJ saw me and a big smile formed on his face. He seemed happy to see us. He came over to our car, and I honestly couldn't believe that he even remembered who I was, much less that he was being so nice. I just couldn't get past the fact that some of my favorite performers in the world were all just a few steps away inside the hotel lobby and that for some reason I was being given the chance to interact with them all! What are the odds? AJ knew all about my desire to meet Tamyra Gray, as that day in the green room at the *Jenny Jones Show*, I'd told him how much I was enjoying the show and how Tamyra's singing had inspired me so much that I had sung the song she had performed on *Jenny Jones*. So when he came over, the first thing he said after he gave me a hug was, "Come on, I want you to meet Tamyra." He dragged me by my arm into the lobby and started introducing me to everyone: Ryan Starr, Jim Verraros, Nikki, Christina Christian, RJ Helton, Ejay Day, and yes, Tamyra Gray! There they were live in person! AJ then asked me to go ahead and sing for them. I couldn't believe what was happening!

After I sang for the first group of Idols, Justin Guarini and Kelly Clarkson arrived and joined the group. At that point, I was in utter awe. My heart was racing, my palms were sweaty, and in that moment I felt that I was very possibly the most nervous kid in the world. But at the same time, I was so excited I had to pinch myself to make sure I wasn't dreaming or imagining the whole scene! "David, sing for them!" AJ said. He turned to Kelly and Justin and said, "You gotta hear this kid sing." And there in the lobby of the Renaissance Hotel, I sang my eleven-year-old guts out to my personal heroes. When the group had gathered, they had a production assistant with them who acted like they were in a big hurry, and as Justin came down the stairs first and entered the lobby, a couple of anxious high school aged girls ran up to him and asked for his autograph. One of them bent over so he could use her back to write on. Meanwhile, Kelly was cheering me on; she wanted to know my name and was as friendly as I had pictured her on TV. We were now beyond *Jenny Jones*—it was more like Cloud Nine.

It seemed that everyone in the whole world that was famous was at that hotel that week, and all the important magazines, newspapers and major television networks were there too. In addition to the *American Idol* finale, there was a big Microsoft meeting of some kind, so Bill Gates was there with two bodyguards and also a bunch of famous guests such as James Cameron, Quincy Jones, Sinbad, and LL Cool J, just to name a few. There was also some kind of Hawaiian Tropic beauty pageant happening nearby, so the hotel was crawling with all kinds of beautiful people in pursuit of their dreams. The energy was electrifying that weekend, and every second that passed felt less and less real. After that very special moment of being able to sing to and meet all the Idols, all I wanted to do was sit in the lobby of what felt like some kind of enchanted hotel. Every so often people would come up and say, "Hey, you're that little kid who sang before! Could you sing again?" I was so happy. It just seemed like the thing to do. So, I just kept on singing in the lobby for groups of random people several times. Every mini-show gave me more and more confidence, and it began to feel that it was my personal duty, my job, to deliver each time. (I felt like it was really important for people to ask though. I wouldn't dare sing unless I felt like I had this kind of permission or acceptance from strangers when they would request a song.) With each little "gig," I would feel more at ease, more comfortable, and more thrilled by the fun of it all.

And just when I thought that things couldn't get any more interesting, my dad decided to reveal part one of his surprise. He said, "David, guess what. I have a little surprise for you. How would you like to hang out here and go to the final performance show tomorrow night?" At first I thought he was playing a trick on me, but when it became clear that he was serious I literally almost passed out. I was so overwhelmed from everything that had already taken place that this just seemed to throw me over the edge. It was beyond icing on the cake, beyond the cherry on top—it was the ultimate surprise for me. The chance to see and hear the finalists live onstage gave me the feeling that I could see into and be a small part of this show that I had been following personally for so many months and that inspired me so much. I felt blessed with good fortune and didn't know what to do to contain my joy and gratitude.

There were actually two shows that week: the performance night and the results show. On the performance night, the two finalists had one last chance to show the audience and the judges why they should be the American Idol. This would be the finale performance for Kelly and Justin, their last chance to give it their all and make a lasting impression before the American public got to place their final votes. We had tickets for the performance night but not the second night; so my dad was now on a mission to get tickets for the final night, which would make the experience complete for me. He had heard a rumor that there might be more tickets available if we got to the box office really early in the morning. In the morning, they went downstairs to the box office next door and ended up being right behind Paula Abdul, who was picking up some tickets for some of her friends and family. We also were able to get tickets for the last night too! What a magical weekend this was turning out to be!

The shows were basically a monumental two-part finale, and I felt beyond lucky to be able to witness even a fraction of it. On performance night, the final ten were reunited for one last show as a group, and then Justin and Kelly, who were the two finalists, sang a duet together before singing the two new songs that each contestant had to sing, "Before Your Love" and "A Moment Like This." All the songs were absolutely spellbinding. You could feel all the performers' emotions swirling around the Kodak Theatre, everyone blazing with nostalgia and joy. I had to keep telling myself that it was real and that this was all actually happening. I was in fact sitting there getting the chance to watch these great performers and be a part of it. The theater lights felt hot on the back of my neck, and I couldn't stop wondering about what might be going through the finalists' minds. The audience was completely alive, with all eyes fixed on the stage. Some people stood up, others just held their hands close to their chest in anticipation; but it was clear that everyone who was there genuinely wanted to be a part of it. I know I was beyond excited to be there. Natalie Cole herself just so happened to be sitting in the audience, which, as you can imagine, was a special treat for me, considering my "history" with her and how much I loved her as an artist.

As I was sitting there in the crowd watching the singers, my mind was racing and I wondered, *How do they feel right now? What did they all do to prepare? How did they choose the arrangements? Did they have any of their family members and friends there in the audience?* It was as if I could feel their excitement as my own, and it was absolutely thrilling. I even wondered if by the time I was sixteen and old enough to even consider auditioning myself, the show and the opportunity would still be there for someone like me. The one thing I did know for sure was that at that moment, just being present to witness this was more than enough. All these unexpected surprises were a total success.

I felt like the luckiest kid on the planet to be there. I think it's safe to say that at that time, *American Idol* was a turning point for me musically; and seeing how a real performer who knew how to sing and make people feel something special got me so excited about wanting to perform and be able to make the same positive impact. Imagine, I had been watching every single episode for the last six months, and I'm just now realizing I might be able to call myself a singer, and now I got to sit in the audience in Los Angeles, partaking of the grand culmination— live in real time! When Kelly Clarkson sang "A Moment Like This," it almost felt like she was singing directly to me. This was it—this was really show time. The show was an amazing showcase of pure talent.

The purpose of the second night was to formally announce the winner, and to look back on some of the highlights from the season. Both nights were loaded with tension, the singers and audience members alike all eager to see the results, and happy to celebrate the journey as a group. The moment that stands out the most in my memory from this night was when they announced Kelly's name, which was followed by this amazing rain of confetti that fell all over us in true celebration style. She was so overcome with emotion! Justin was such a gentleman and sincerely looked happy for her. I remember noticing his reaction and thinking that his demeanor was very cool and dignified. It sort of stripped the whole "winning" thing away from a very special moment, and instead made it one where they could both be a part of it as friends.

When the results show was over, we were walking through the Kodak Theatre breezeway, which led back to our room at the Renaissance Hotel, when someone called out my dad's name. He didn't respond at first because who would be calling for us there? We heard it again, and looked over and I recognized that it was someone I was sitting next to during the finale. I didn't even realize that it was the son of the guy in Las Vegas who had sold us the tickets; I guess they'd simply had four tickets. He had sold two to us and given two to his son. The son was probably either just out of college or maybe even still in high school and was really nice. He had remembered my singing and asked if I would sing again for him and his friends. By now, energized with all that happened over the last few days, I was more comfortable with the idea of singing to people who were nice enough to ask.

And here's where it got really exciting for me: I didn't realize that the place where we were standing was right next to where the judges were going to walk by. It turned out to be a space set aside for them to speak to the press, so there were tons of camera crews and reporters out there to watch the big results of the finale.

With my back toward the camera crews and reporters, not realizing what was going on behind me, I started singing for our new friends. I was totally unaware of the scene that was quickly brewing around us. Reporters asked my dad who I was and where we were from. And as I was singing some of the cameramen were looking toward where the judges were supposed to be coming, then looking at me, then looking at the interview people, then back, not sure what they should do. Finally, a lady from FOX had the camera guy she was working with turn around and start filming me while I was singing to our new friends. Then, as I got near the end of the song, everyone started pointing behind me and telling me to turn around because right then and there, the three *Idol* judges, Simon, Paula and Randy, all came out. Just as I was belting out the last line of the song, which happened to be "You're Gonna Love Me," Paula, surrounded by an entourage of makeup people and publicists, stopped and looked right at me and said, "I'm gonna love you!" The word "surreal" could not even begin to describe how things were starting to feel at this point. Never mind that I had just been hugged by Paula Abdul herself in the hallway behind the Kodak Theatre in Los Angeles on the heels of the *Idol* finale; but just as crazy was all the people and reporters and the cameras and the electricity that was there! It was almost overwhelming. Right after that happened, a producer from *Good Morning America* asked if they could interview me for their *Idol* segment that was going to be taped in half an hour. Someone else from *The Pulse* came over and asked if I could do their show! We couldn't believe what was happening. We were just there to watch the show, totally unprepared for the crazy whirlwind that seemed to be hitting us out of nowhere.

The next thing I knew, I was sitting in a FOX Television booth in a director's chair, sitting in front of the logo I had become very familiar with over the past several weeks, the one that says *American Idol* with a purple background. The producer gave my dad her card and told him that her own father, Sandy Linzer, was a songwriter. When my dad looked him up, sure enough, we found out he wrote the song "I Believe in You and Me," which was another song I really loved. She even said we could call him if we ever had any questions. It just seemed that everything was happening in this very lucky and magical way; the planets and stars were lining up in our favor.

The *American Idol* adventure, or what my family and I refer to as "The Magical Weekend," was without a doubt the coolest thing that I had ever been a part of (and remember that this was when I was just an audience member and fan of the show). Our whole family was on a total high from the events that took place in Los Angeles. They all felt great that we had received real validation from so many different people in the industry. It was one thing for our friends and family to love my singing, but now total strangers, media, and even music professionals were responding more positively than any of us could have ever hoped for. It felt like things were very naturally and organically moving in the right direction.

In fact, one talent manager who had introduced herself to my dad the night of the show came up to our suite the very next morning and told us that she had lined up a bunch of meetings for us with A&R (artists and repertoire) people and several publicists in both L.A. and New York. Among the appointments she had arranged in L.A. was a meeting with Magic Johnson's record label and another guy who originally signed Pink. As for New York, we had appointments at the Sony building with Dave McPherson, who signed Britney Spears and the Backstreet Boys to Epic Records. Then we had a meeting with a guy named Jeff Fenster from Def Jam records. He had been referred to us by LL Cool J's A&R rep after he overheard me sing in the lobby. I wish I had been old enough to understand just how epic all of this really was. The simple truth is that I didn't really get it. I was just a kid who loved to sing. But can you imagine? First Chicago, then Los Angeles, and now New York City!

After the crazy whirlwind of L.A., my father and I flew out to New York and spent a whole week there meeting with all kinds of industry people. We were hoping that being face-to-face with record label executives would give us a better understanding and a clearer picture going forward. After all, my dad comes from the jazz world, which is a completely different scene than the pop world. And if he was confused about what to do, imagine how clueless I was.

At that age, I probably knew more about Pokémon and dinosaurs than I knew about music experience. I mean, yes, it was totally exciting to sit in a Manhattan skyscraper in a room full of framed gold records and seeing all these signed posters of people who I admired for their music. It was definitely exciting, but equally intimidating. I felt tiny in the middle of it all and could barely get a word out to anyone who tried to engage me because I was still a really shy boy. The execs asked me what kind of music I liked and my answer would be something like: "Um . . . all kinds" or "Lots." I just couldn't really communicate back then (unless I was singing). I guess I was still pretty shy and self-conscious. I was clearly not ready to articulate or express my feelings about music, nor was I sure that I even knew what my goals were, beyond just singing. I had zero motivation for things like fame or recognition. I mean, come on, how many eleven-year-olds do you know who already have life plans? All I wanted to do was just sing.

All the people we met said that I had talent, but none of them could figure out just what to do with me. I remember one of the meetings was with a Sony executive right in the heart of Times Square. "David," he said, "there is no question that you have talent, but in all sincerity, I don't know what to do with you. You're a little white kid from Utah who sings with the soul of a black R & B singer who grew up in the gospel world. But I think you're too young right now. Here's what I suggest: Learn how to play some instruments and learn how to write." He, like most of the people we met, said that if I did all of these things, by the time I was old enough for anything serious to happen, I would be better prepared to take it all on with a more focused approach. They also kept reminding me that my voice still hadn't gone through "the change" yet either. So right now, I was simply too much of a kid to make anything happen. (Coincidentally, we also had a meeting at Def Jam with Jeff Fenster, who years later would end up becoming my A & R rep at Jive Records. So even though I was too young then for anything to really happen, I guess the seeds were somehow being planted!)

We decided to go back home and try to follow some of the advice we were given in New York. I started to play the piano again, something I hadn't really done since we left Florida because we didn't have a piano when we first got to Utah. My playing felt rusty and unsophisticated compared to some of the kids in my neighborhood who had studied for years with a well-known teacher and now played at a very high level. I felt I had so much catching up to do and didn't feel I could compete. My parents would tell me not to compare myself and reminded me that this was part of the process and not to worry, I was really young and had plenty of time to just have fun learning as much as I could about notes and words and music.

I had no choice but to sit tight and continue developing myself as a singer with no expectations. I knew that something important was starting to brew. That year was magically bizarre: I went from crying my eyes out backstage at the Utah talent show, to meeting AJ Gil at the *Jenny Jones Show*, to singing for Natalie Cole, Tamyra Gray and Kelly Clarkson (and a bunch of other strangers all over L.A.), to seeing the first-ever finale of *Idol* live, to taking meetings up on a top floor of a New York City skyscraper. I couldn't understand how or why this was happening and how I got to experience it all. It's just me, just David. But at the same time I knew I also had to start believing that it was all happening for a reason. What the reason was, I had no idea, but I knew that I was going to keep trusting, keep the faith, and go with the flow. If nothing else, at least I felt a bit more comfortable about the idea of walking onto a stage and that I did not have to be afraid of it, and that meant the beginning of all kinds of possibilities.

Courtesy of the author

Learning to play an instrument definitely allowed me to connect with songs on a deeper level.

BUMPS IN THE ROAD

"Most great people have attained their greatest success just one step beyond their greatest failure."

—NAPOLEON HILL

4

Very soon after we returned from New York, we got a phone call from one of our new friends, Diane, who we had met in California. She said they were bringing back the show *Star Search* and were having auditions coming up in November, and she encouraged us to come down. We gave it some thought and in the end decided it would be a good idea. So two months after part one of the crazy Los Angeles whirlwind, we headed back for what would be part two. I went on my audition with a little more confidence than I'd had before and it seemed to go well, but this time I didn't get a call back. I wasn't upset or anything; in fact, I wasn't surprised because I believed what they had told me in New York about being too young and inexperienced. Some of the other kids were really

I was probably 13 here, at an event

Victor Spinelli/ Wire Image / Getty Images

impressive and some of them even already had managers and vocal coaches with them. I felt like I was perhaps out of my league, but by now, my dad thought differently. He was confident that I was good enough and tried to reassure me, but in my mind, I just knew I wasn't good enough yet to compete with a lot of the talent out there. I felt I was always very realistic and didn't kid myself about my limitations.

Anyway, the new 2002 version of *Star Search* had Arsenio Hall as the host, along with house judges Ben Stein, Naomi Judd, and a special guest judge. This CBS revival would include four series the first year, and a single series the second year. During the first three series, two new competitors would face off in each category (which were Adult Singer, Junior Singer, Comedy, Dance and Modeling). The three judges and one celebrity guest judge would give each contestant a score from one to five stars, for a maximum score of twenty. During the commercial breaks, the home audience could go online to rate the competitors who'd just performed, which allowed each performer to earn up to another twenty stars. "Hit me with the digits!" Arsenio would holler just as the results of each home audience score were about to be revealed. When the scores were tallied, the performer with the higher score would be the winner of that category. If it was a tie, Arsenio would read off each performer's score rounded to the nearest hundredth. That performer would then go on to the next round of competition. After the first three series, a fourth one called "Battle of the Champions" took place, where the winners of each category were brought back to compete for a single show; winner takes all $100,000 cash prize.

It was a fresh start to an old show, keeping the spirit of *Idol*. In fact, *Star Search* kicked off at the same time as *Idol*'s second season. I remember watching and understanding clearly why I hadn't made the cut. These kids were amazing, belting out tunes like grown adults who already knew things about music that intimidated me and made me feel glad I didn't get called back just to be embarrassed! We watched the first whole five-week season totally impressed by the diversity of talent, awed by the range the young contestants all seemed to show. I was amazed at how many wonderful singers there were out there and blown away by the way they were able to relate to the songs they were singing. They seemed like complete professionals out there, charged with the kind of confidence I'd always wished for. It was both inspiring and humbling, which definitely helped me realize that if I wanted to get to that level, I would need to start working really hard.

But things never happen exactly how you think they will, because, out of nowhere, as the season wrapped up we got a call from Seth Riggs, who had been hired by CBS to work with the contestants in the *Star Search* finale. He told us that a second season was already in the works and that he had been asked to refer some new talent for that cycle. He recommended me, and shortly afterward we got a call asking for a video of me singing. We quickly sent it in and had to send in two more videos until, to our surprise and excitement, we got the green light: They wanted me on the show for the second season! Within three days we were back in L.A.

I honestly feel that the whole *Star Search* thing was able to happen at all because of how much *Idol* influenced me, which is why I like to joke that I was trained in the "School of *American Idol*." By featuring so many different types of people trying to tackle such a wide range of songs on the show, I think *Idol* gave us a mini–crash course in musicology, which broadened my sense of what kinds of songs to sing and expanded my idea of how to individualize music. But, of course, I was still very much afraid and full of self-doubt, because I didn't think I was as good a singer as the kids I'd seen perform on the show. Though I had sung for many audiences, not since *Jenny Jones* had I performed for a television audience, and I felt there was a serious risk of humiliating myself.

This would be our third trip to California and it started to feel like L.A. was our home away from home. Although I felt scared every time, each visit made me feel more and more excited about my desire to become a better singer. I tried to remember to always see my performances as opportunities to get better and share my talent. And even though I was afraid, once I started to sing, I'd go into some kind of peaceful, stress-free state where all that mattered was the sound of the music and the feelings that it carried. Those feelings would always overpower any fear that crept up.

Another uncomfortable feeling I had to deal with was the feeling of guilt when someone I thought of as more talented than me would lose out. For example, there were three kids auditioning for *Star Search* with me, and only two of us would get chosen for the show. I was sure I wouldn't make it but I did. Now I felt terrible, because I really thought one of the others was a lot better than me. Then I saw her crying and it kind of broke my heart. I just couldn't shake this feeling that I might have taken something away from someone who deserved it more. I couldn't handle how sad that poor girl was. I knew she had worked just as hard as I had. I never felt like I was good enough to win and almost felt embarrassed when I did. In a way, I didn't even think I belonged there to begin with. I loved singing so much, but when that meant competing and beating out other people, that's when it got a bit weird for me. It has nothing to do with humility; I just saw it as unfair.

But I would try to shake off these nagging negative feelings, and instead focus on the idea that this was all part of my training and education as a lover of music and aspiring singer. For the preliminary round, I chose to sing The Jackson 5's "Who's Loving You?" I remember Hilary Duff was the guest judge, and she smiled so sweetly throughout my entire song. The person I was competing against was Anna Maria Perez de Tagle who later was on *Hannah Montana* and in the movie *Camp Rock*. Then for the semifinal round, I was up against two girls, Joelle James who made the Top 24 on season six of *Idol*, and Tori Kelly who just barely didn't make it to the Top 24 but made it through Hollywood Week of season nine. They both were so amazing; I knew I didn't have a chance to make it through to the final, but I figured I'd just give it my best. I picked for my song, "Fallin'" by Alicia Keyes and tried to put my own twist on it. Joelle was amazing, but she was sick that week and I felt really bad for her that she wasn't at 100%, but she still sounded amazing singing "Ain't No Mountain High Enough." Tori then sang the song "Blessed" by Rachel Lampa, and I figured I had had a great time and wasn't going to feel bad if I didn't make it past the semi. When the voting came in after commercial break, the scores were so close that Tori and I actually tied. It came down to fractions, and when the final tally came in, I had won by less than two-tenths of a point! I couldn't believe it! Could this have really happened? Did I really deserve to be the one moving on? I was extremely happy, but I felt like something had gone wrong. There was no way I should have been able to beat them both. After the semi, I found out I was going to be in the finals against a girl named Molly. I chose the song "You're All I Need to Get By" which I first heard Kelly Clarkson sing on *American Idol*. I later found out that it was performed by Marvin Gaye and Tammi Terrell and that

things never happen exactly how you think they will

Aretha Franklin had also recorded it. My dad and I worked out an arrangement that combined some ideas from both versions as well as some original ideas that would make the song my own. I felt it was my best performance and I really had a great time putting my all into it decked out in my then favorite leather jacket! When the final scores came back, I couldn't believe that I had won! I got straight 5s from the judges and it was my chance to feel I had achieved a dream that was unimaginable just a few weeks earlier when I was sitting at home watching in amazement the very same people I had competed against, and now having to pinch myself because somehow I had become the Junior Vocal champion.

But what might have been a celebration was quickly stunted by the news of the Iraq War. All regular television programming was interrupted and the networks collectively switched to news coverage. So really not many people got to hear me sing that night, and there was no special party or celebration after the winner was crowned.

The night of my final appearance happened to be the same night the Iraqi war started. As a result, they ended our show after the junior vocals and dancers had performed, and the show wasn't even aired for most of the country. So unless you lived on the east coast, you probably would not have seen my final performance. The final episode of our season ended as part of the first show of the third season, which sounds confusing, but because they had to cut the show short previously, they had to combine the last part of the show with the first show of season three. It was the only way they could make it work. After the third season was over, they called us back to be part of a special one night "Battle of the Champions" episode. They had the three winners from each previous cycle to compete for another $100,000. It was back to Los Angeles again for us. We were starting to really get comfortable with the routine and understood that being a singer would include a lot of travel and hectic moving around. It was exciting and exhausting, but it was a lot of fun. I got to know the other kids very well as we went to school every day on the set and had a great time getting to know one another. We had all already won our season, so none of us really felt like it was a competition, but more of a chance to sing one last time. I chose to sing "I Surrender" by Celine Dion for this round, and though I was not expecting to do well at all, I managed to get some great comments from the judges even though I didn't win. I managed to end up as the Junior Vocal Champion on *Star Search 2*, losing the Junior Grand Champion "Battle of the Champions" title to Tiffany Evans. She was over-the-top amazing and I saw it as a good thing that I hadn't won, because in all honesty I couldn't imagine winning against her. It felt great just to be considered at her level, and the chance to sing with her once again was totally flattering to me.

In fact, even though I sang okay that night, I kind of knew I wasn't going to win. I wasn't disappointed because I knew that I'd given it my all but just wasn't the best singer there. So was I sad or bummed out? It was never about winning for me. What I cared about was just having one more opportunity to share my talent and perform. Two years earlier in Utah, I was terrified to walk onto a stage, and here I was in Hollywood, much more calm and excited every time I held a microphone in my hand. Not a bad result!

After *Star Search* finished in May, we stayed in Hollywood for a few weeks, and I recorded a demo version of my first song written for me by my dad and an amazing songwriter friend, Sunny Hilden (another friend we met during that magical weekend of the *Idol* finale), called "Dream Sky High." It was an inspirational song about angels, and I really enjoyed singing it. We also had a chance to meet with several attorneys and producers to learn a little more about the music business and see if having won *Star Search* would open any new doors for me. It still seemed that I was probably not quite ready to actually try to get a record deal so we went home. I went back to school for my sixth-grade year and prepared to start my next school year in seventh grade. While I was home for the summer just being a normal kid, I got really sick one night and found out that I had appendicitis. I remember how much pain I felt and how at first my parents thought I just had a bad stomachache or the flu. By nighttime, I had a high fever and so much pain that I was rushed to the hospital. I had my appendix removed successfully and then had to go home for bed rest right when my seventh grade was supposed to start. I finally started school at a new charter school called American Preparatory Academy with my sisters Claudia and Jazzy and my brother Daniel. We really enjoyed that school and felt we learned a lot there. It was a very positive environment and had a lot of great kids going there as well as some great teachers.

STAR SEARCH SONGS

PRELIMINARY ROUND
"Who's Loving You" by Jackson 5

SEMIFINALS
"Fallin'" by Alicia Keys

FINALS
"You're All I Need to Get By" by Marvin Gaye

BATTLE OF THE CHAMPIONS
"I Surrender" by Celine Dion

SECOND-YEAR WINNER'S CIRCLE
"A House Is Not a Home" by Luther Vandross
"Climb Every Mountain" from *The Sound of Music*
"Ain't No Sunshine" by Bill Withers
"Get Here" by Oleta Adams
"Wind Beneath My Wings" by Bette Midler

Sometime around Thanksgiving, after only being back to school for a few months, my dad received a phone call from the people at *Star Search* asking if I could come back for a special show they were putting together for the new season. For this would come to be the final *Star Search* series, three winners from the previous year or sometimes a contestant who was a runner-up were brought back to compete. Mark Mejia, Molly, and I were the three Junior Vocalists. By then, the show had decided to just have three judges now on the panel; fifteen stars was the highest score possible. The winner had the chance to challenge another performer. The one challenged had to beat or tie the challenger. If they couldn't, they were out of the competition, and the challenger took his or her place in the winners' circle. Halfway through the series, the three performers in each winners' circle competed against one another in a special show.

When I arrived in Hollywood for the second year of *Star Search*, I was sick with a pretty bad cold, which was an ongoing battle for me during my early years in singing. I had come down with the kind of cold that I'd always get around Christmas. It wasn't my greatest year health-wise; I'd had bronchitis over the summer, which I hadn't fully recovered from, and in the fall, I had appendicitis and had my appendix removed. Now I had this chronic cold, where I'd get all stuffy and a little weak. It wasn't a big deal, I was pretty used to it by now, and I never thought it was anything to worry about. People get sick during the winter, right? But it got worse and worse while I was on *Star Search*, until by the sixth week, I could barely get through a song. At first, we thought maybe it was that my voice was starting to change, but we also knew very well that this usually doesn't affect a person's breathing. I was so wheezy and short of breath that even my talking became restricted, and I couldn't sing for more than ten or fifteen minutes without getting really worn out and having a hard time controlling my pitch or holding out a note for very long. I hadn't ever had this extreme of a problem before and my family was nervous about what was happening, but I guess I was a bit in denial of (or just too young to understand) what this could mean.

I knew that the other kids competing were able to hear me sing, and I was starting to really suffer thinking about how I must've sounded. I don't know how, but I kept going to the next round with each cycle, and I even believed they kept picking me on the show out of mercy because they felt bad that I was so sick. I mean, I knew I sounded like I had a problem, and it had to be obvious to everyone else listening as well.

One night my dad sat with me and said, "David, you may have a medical condition. Do you still want to sing tonight? Or should we just talk to the show people and tell them that we should withdraw?" I thought about it for a while and my reply was, "Dad, I don't care if I lose or win, I just want to have one last chance to try." I sang my song for week 6, and I guess I sounded okay; but my belief in myself was starting to dwindle slightly, and my ability to stay as strong as I could was also starting to fade. This was obviously not a regular cold and whatever it was, we didn't want to make it worse. It was time to see a specialist.

I really had a great time putting my all into it

The doctor said that they would have to use an endoscope (a type of camera that they run through the nasal passage) to see what was going on. "Very interesting," he said. "What I am seeing is really not normal for a child. It's usually something we see in our elderly patients." He showed us the video of my vocal cords, and we could clearly see that only one of them was vibrating when I spoke or tried to sing; the other was barely moving. The doctor said it looked partially paralyzed, which could have come from a virus I may have caught when I had bronchitis. The good news was that it was not completely paralyzed, because if it had been, I would be getting no sound at all. At least now, we understood why I had to work so hard when I sang, but I was crushed. When you're someone who loves to sing, "vocal paralysis" are not words you ever want to hear.

Especially discouraging was the fact that there wasn't much we could do about it. Our two options were basically high-risk surgery that could permanently mess up my ability to sing or vocal therapy that would slowly rehabilitate the damaged cord. That sounded kind of vague and wishy-washy to me, but the surgery sounded even worse. That was the only thing I could do. The surgery was out of the question.

After *Star Search* and the news of my diagnosis, we hung out in Hollywood for a couple of weeks, meeting with producers and song-writers. *Star Search* had opened a lot of doors, and we tried to be as productive as possible while things were fresh in people's minds. We must have met with six or seven different lawyers just to try to learn how things work. People were so helpful, considerate and kind to me, but still, no one seemed to know what to do with me. I still wasn't able to communicate verbally what I wanted to do musically, and so there was no clear sense of direction for us to take.

There were times in L.A. when my dad would ask me to sing, or talk to some executive about singing, and I just couldn't get the words out. Maybe I was overwhelmed by everything, or maybe I really was just too young to get it—but there were many moments where I was at a total loss for what to say. My personality wasn't yet fully developed, and the only way I knew to truly let go was when I was singing onstage. But you can't sing for every single second of your life, can you?

When everything simmered down in California, we went back home where, despite my new diagnosis, I continued to have a few local opportunities to sing. The doctors never told me not to sing, so I sang at our church, and at a few special events. I did the best I could, and simply tried to avoid singing for extended sets. I remember one show at Pioneer Day, which is a state holiday in Utah and kind of like the Fourth of July. The show producers put together some custom arrangements for me, including an orchestral version of "Dream Sky High" with a full-blown orchestra and a background choir. The event itself was held in this grand and elegant hall in Salt Lake, Abravenal Hall. I walked onstage in my tuxedo and sang several songs including "Joyful, Joyful," "Down by the River to Pray," and, of course, "Dream Sky High," trying to enjoy the moment but knowing deep down that my voice wasn't what it used to be.

I tried to keep up with my singing as much as I could, but now I was thirteen and getting older, so I was also starting to think about the rest of my life. I couldn't do more than one or two songs in any performance, and it seriously bummed me out. I didn't think I could force my voice to work the way I wanted it to. Sometimes you just have to accept things the way they are, I told myself.

Here I am singing at a wedding in Utah

I continued with my vocal therapy exercises. I'd go to my voice lessons for a while, and then I'd stop, feeling like the whole thing was a waste of time and that I'd never be able to sing like I used to. My situation was like someone who's suffered a stroke and needs to retrain certain muscles how to work. I literally needed to train my paralyzed vocal cord how to vibrate again. I did special exercises that helped strengthen the vocal cord little by little, and I learned to turn my head to one side while I sang, to relieve the cord that was doing all the work and to be sure the weak cord was having to vibrate. That seemed to help a little, but it was hard not to feel negative or discouraged at times. Sometimes I thought the whole therapy thing was going nowhere. Other times, I thought, maybe it will work; let's keep giving it a shot. But all in all, I wasn't too hopeful; I was starting to give up.

I thought, how could I possibly be a serious singer with a paralyzed vocal cord that will only get worse with time? Singing was getting harder and harder to do. I didn't have the energy I used to have when I was eleven—I figured I'd have to come up with other ways to make my life meaningful and complete. But up until now, besides family and friends, music was pretty much the only thing I ever wanted. From the moment, I got the diagnosis, life quickly went from *Star Search* to soul search.

At school, I tried to be a normal kid. I wanted to be as unassuming as possible and simply have a life like all the rest of the kids around me. I just wanted to be normal. I would do little gigs here and there, but I was starting to treat it more like a hobby that I loved and less like a career path. It was almost time to start high school and I was excited to get to hang out with my friends and just do what other kids my age do. I started to focus on getting good grades and learning as much as I could so that I could make clear decisions when it was time for college.

From ninth through eleventh grades I just assumed the singing part of my life was over. I found a way to accept it by trying to be a bit more social and to even start brainstorming about what kind of direction I would take after school. I knew the SAT tests would be coming, so studying would certainly take some time and energy. I wanted to do well so that I could have real options down the line. There were so many subjects that were interesting to me, and there would soon come a time when I would have to make decisions about college and majors—things that I was really looking forward to and wanted to take as seriously as I did my singing.

Between eighth grade and ninth grade, I rediscovered running, which was an activity that always made me feel relaxed and peaceful as well as made my body feel good. I would run all the way from the house to school and I'd keep going on the track there. Running calmed me down and in general it was a great way to relieve stress. That summer, while I was running at the high school track, I was approached by the cross country coach who invited me to just come work out with his team. He said that as a ninth grader, I could even participate in the meets if I wanted to. I met with them for a party, which meant we were going to go up the canyon and run, then meet at the bottom of the canyon and have a bonfire and just get to know one another as a team. I really enjoyed that, and during ninth grade, I did participate in the high school meets. I continued running on my own a bit, but after ninth grade, I decided not to continue once I was actually in high school.

> **I wanted to be as unassuming as possible and simply have a life like all the rest of the kids around me.**

But I couldn't kid myself too much. Though I was having fun at school with my friends, it was also kind of depressing because I felt like I had somehow lost a little piece of my identity. I had spent a good part of my childhood with a microphone in my hand, and now I felt kind of useless. I started to wonder if maybe it was a test from God; maybe

He wanted to see how strong I was, how open-minded I could be when faced with obstacles that were out of my control. With that in mind, I tried as hard as I could to see the bright side of things by being grateful for the fact that at least both of my vocal cords were not damaged, and that thankfully, I could still speak and sing a song or two now and again. I wanted to be optimistic. But very often, it was hard to find that bright side. I guess I saw it as a sign that singing maybe wasn't my path. You know what they say: Maybe it just wasn't meant to be.

HOPE RISES

"The pessimist sees difficulty in every opportunity. The optimist sees the opportunity in every difficulty."

—WINSTON CHURCHILL

CHAPTER

5

Sometimes it takes a miracle to reignite a person's passion. Sometimes when you least expect it, the tables turn and that scary feeling that has taken hold of you for so long somehow turns into hope. Call it luck, call it help from above, call it whatever you will. As for me, I definitely believe some kind of miracle was at play when my voice, for no understandable or explainable reason, started to gradually feel better again over the period of a year or so from tenth grade to the eleventh grade. Maybe the vocal exercises and just taking it a lot easier vocally had made a difference after all. All I know is that when I tried to sing, I didn't have to work so hard. My sound was freer, my pitch was improving dramatically and my overall sense of control was getting back to where it was supposed to be.

I had been able to sing off and on during the previous few years, but only for short periods of time. I would get tired after just a few minutes and this continued for a year or so. But at a certain point, it seemed that gradually I was feeling better and better. After I was about fifteen or so, it suddenly felt like my voice was getting stronger and I could sing several songs at a time. I even started doing gigs again like singing at a wedding for one of my friend's sister and also for a corporate event that I was going to have to sing for about an hour.

I was still taking it slow because after all those years with "my condition," I felt that I'd gotten rusty, and I no longer had the confidence I'd had after the validation we'd gotten at the *Idol* finale and throughout all the *Star Search* shows. In many ways, I was afraid to sing, or maybe afraid that I would remember just how much I loved to. When I look back, I think I was scared of rekindling this passion because I didn't want to have to let it go again. I didn't want to set myself up for that kind of personal disappointment, and by now the truth is that I was okay with just being a normal kid. If I was naive about singing at age eleven, at age sixteen, it just made me anxious. But I was still grateful for the fact that I didn't have to suffer through a song anymore—even if I was just singing in the shower.

Slowly but surely I started to sing again, just to test myself to see how much I could handle. Though the feelings that came up when I sang were still the same as they had always been, the process was a little different because my voice had lowered quite a bit and I was working with a new kind of sound. My taste had also evolved over the years and now I could sing songs by male vocalists that were more mature as I now had a more tenor range to my voice. There were also all these new genres I was exploring, so while I was still hesitant to sing full out, I have to admit that there was also a part of me that really wanted to dive back in. But you know how it is when you're a teenager: One minute you're super-excited about something, and the next minute you're doubting the exact same thing. But when you know something you can't just "un-know" it, and the one thing I knew for sure was that nothing filled that void, that feeling, that I got from singing. All setbacks aside—insecurity, vocal paralysis and age (to name a few)—I still loved music and I felt that it was time for me to figure out a way to get back into it. I still felt a connection to it that was deeper than any of the setbacks themselves. I couldn't think of anything else in the world that I cared about more, and every time I would think about my purpose, the answers seemed to come in sounds. In melodies. In feelings. There was no escaping the fact that the music was still after me. When it came down to it, it was really very simple: I would rather sing than not sing.

At that point, we all decided it would be good to test the waters again by accepting a full-set gig. It had been three years since I'd sung more than a song or two at a time. Three years since I went for it with a full set, and three years since I felt confident enough to do so. I was out of practice and believed that any return to singing would pretty much mean having to start from scratch. Did I have the energy to do it all over again? After giving it a lot of thought and really trying to figure out if this was a door I wanted to reopen, I made a choice. I decided that this was one of those moments in life when I would have to choose optimism. I forced myself back into the saddle by agreeing to sing a full set of songs for a local performance. I didn't know what to expect, but I made a commitment to do my absolute best. I figured that if I gave it my best and things didn't work out, at least my conscience would be clear that it wasn't for lack of effort. My part, I thought, would be to try my hardest and be as positive as I could. Even though everything else felt a bit like a wild card, my intention to give it my all was the one variable that I could control.

My dad helped me work on the arrangements for the songs and also ran sound for me, and Richard, a friend of ours, came along to play the keyboards. I would start each number by telling the audience a bit about the song and what it meant to me. This was a way of connecting more with the crowd, but also a quick way to help get me in the mindset of the songs' emotional essence. My dad helped me write out an outline of my ideas, and for the first time onstage I felt that I was no longer seeing my audience through the eyes of a child. I was a little older, a little less naive, and a little clearer about just how much music meant to me. After the whole vocal cord issue, I had a brand-new appreciation for what it means to be able to get up there and sing.

I felt pretty good after the gig and was happy I made it through the whole set and that my voice didn't wear out. Somehow, the hardest part was not the singing but having to talk in between the songs. The audience couldn't have been better though, and they even laughed at a lot of what I was saying although I never thought I was trying to be funny. I think I just have a dry sense of humor that comes through sometimes, and it seemed to that day. I felt natural and calm, unlike the early days when it would often feel like I couldn't hear the music over the thump of my own heart. The audience's response was extremely positive. It felt like they were seeing me not as a cute little boy with a good voice but more as a skilled singer with interesting potential. I was happy with how things went, grateful for my recovery and excited about the fact that I didn't have to suppress my love of singing anymore. I felt happy and hopeful that the door I'd chosen to reopen might lead me to something nice.

Seeing the many smiles and shining eyes in the crowd that day was a small infusion of encouragement at a time when I needed it most, because a couple of months later, we realized three very interesting things: *American Idol* was still on, now in its sixth cycle; I was sixteen and finally old enough to try out; and the auditions for the seventh season were just around the corner and taking place in San Diego. I found myself in a very strange situation. Now that I was finally sixteen, you'd have thought I'd jump all over the chance to get on the show. I'm sure many people in my life imagined that I would want to be the first in line. But in fact it was the total opposite. I hadn't been counting the days in anticipation of this moment. After all those years of being told that I was too young to start a career in music, and then my vocal cord being paralyzed, I had accepted a new reality. After everything that happened (or didn't happen), I had accepted that maybe singing just wasn't for me after all and I should just move on to something more practical like becoming an ear, nose, and throat specialist.

My parents didn't push me at all; instead they put the idea out there and let me know that they would help support me if I felt it was something I wanted to do. They would gently remind me of how obsessive I used to be about singing when I was younger, and about the whole crazy L.A. experience with the finalists and Paula Abdul and New York—all of the mayhem of that time. I distinctly remember one conversation when I said, "Mom, what should I do with my life? I know I'm supposed to be in music. But I'm not sure how." The wonderful mom that she is, she just encouraged me and told me that if I really believed in music, I should follow my gut.

Don't get me wrong: I still loved singing as much as I ever had, but love doesn't necessarily equal confidence, and it certainly didn't in my case. I was afraid to try, afraid of what I would sound like now as a teenager, a bit out of practice after so much time thinking that singing was a dead end. I knew that to be on a show like *American Idol*, you really had to be able to sing. I thought it would be a complete waste of time. Why should I go out there just to be rejected?

But it was not just my parents who were encouraging me to audition. Friends and other relatives, too, started to put the bug in my ear, and even though I tried to ignore them all, I have to admit that the question of whether to go or not started to nag at me a bit. I really tried to push the whole thing out of my mind, but for some reason, I just couldn't. When someone would ask me if I was planning to go, I'd instantly say no; but as each day passed that "no" would gradually start to blur a bit, confusing me about what the answer should really be. I'm not entirely sure why, but some part of me started to think about the possibility of giving it a go. Maybe it was my instinct or some inner voice, I don't know—but there just wasn't any getting away from the feeling that these auditions were somehow calling my name.

My father offered to help me research song options and prepare the arrangements as he always had in the past. But I was still in denial about the whole thing and would dodge these conversations or find some other way to blow it all off. I just couldn't get past the fact that so much time had passed since my days on *Jenny Jones* and *Star Search*. Wasn't I just a washed-up kid singer with a vocal problem?

My dad felt it might be good to make a few calls to some of the contacts we had made in Hollywood during the *Star Search* experience to help us get some perspective. What did they think would be best, should I maybe just try it on my own, or would it make sense to try *Idol* as a vehicle to get some exposure perhaps? Just as I expected, they pretty much discouraged us, saying that it was VERY hard these days to get a deal and that it required an established fan base to get a label to look at you unless you were already on a TV show or were in a movie. They said that *Star Search* was old news; that our winning moments happened years ago when I was a lot younger and that people would respond differently to me now that I was a totally different person. They didn't believe that I was relevant anymore, and neither did I. I even thought that maybe I'd only won in the past because I was a kid.

my intention to give it my all was the one variable that I could control

And that wasn't my only problem: That summer I had taken my first job. I was hired as a sound tech at the Murray Park Amphitheater—a responsibility that I didn't take for granted and actually considered to be pretty important. To even think about going on the audition, I had to approach my bosses and see how they'd feel about me taking some time off. Needless to say, they were not into it at all and basically told me that if I left it would be pretty certain that I would be out of a job. They were nice, but they were also honest. I get the fact that people are expendable; so I felt that I should hold on to what I had and not get too caught up in an illusion. As I weighed the pros and cons, it just didn't seem rational to leave my job for something that probably wouldn't work out anyway. If I left my job to go try out and didn't get in, it would be a waste of time, plus I would have to find another job. I liked that job; it was a lot of fun, and I worked with all my friends. I'd worked hard to get it. Was it really worth the risk?

Having a job meant having purpose, which was something that I took seriously and was proud to finally be able to do. I was learning a lot, earning a bit of money on my own, and feeling like I was slowly but surely finally starting to grow up. How could I just pick up and go to San Diego and abandon my new responsibility? I wasn't a little child anymore and I was actually accountable for something. That felt good; it felt empowering. Going to the auditions would mean not only losing my job but spending money on flights and hotels. It seemed like a high price to pay (morally and financially) at a time when I no longer even thought of myself as a "real" singer. I didn't believe that I would get very far, nor did I have dreams of one day being a pop star. I just didn't see the point of trying out.

But every day that passed was another day closer to the auditions, and I still couldn't seem to shake that nagging feeling. Something deep inside was trying to make a point, and after many days and nights of battling the question of whether I should go or not, I chose to do the only thing that I knew would help me decide: I prayed. It was clear that I wasn't going to be able to come to the decision on my own, so I surrendered to the uncertainty and humbly asked for help. Even though I was literally asking God if I should try out for *American Idol*, I think what I was really asking is if He still believed in me. I needed to have that moment with God to look inward and honestly confront my deepest motivations, my dreams and my purpose as a person. I felt that I needed some kind of validation, besides the urging of all the people around me, that this was the right thing to do. I had to look deep, I had to ask the basic questions and I had to turn to God for help. And that night I was happy and grateful to discover that He was definitely listening.

I knelt by my bed, closed my eyes and talked to him the only way I knew how: calmly, simply and honestly. I didn't make a big fuss, and I didn't get all dramatic about it. I just laid out my questions as openly as I possibly could. At first I felt a bit silly to be praying about something as unimportant as a TV show, because I didn't want to bother him with something that seemed rather trivial compared to all the other problems in the world. It's not like I expected a giant hand to come down from the sky and spell out a "yes" or "no" in big blazing letters. But still, slowly but surely, I felt uncertainty about my question starting to come into focus. I don't know how else to describe it, but I felt an overwhelming sense that I did have to go to the audition in San Diego. It wasn't something that I could even describe in words—it was more like an overpowering feeling, the kind you can't really argue with. I didn't understand in any intellectual or rational way why I needed to do it, but I just deeply felt that I should.

I realized through this comforting and pure feeling that God does care about me, and that by giving me an answer, He was acknowledging my potential. Despite the odds, I felt strongly that I had to go. Even if I failed, I thought to myself that maybe there is something that I need to learn from going. I guess I just have to have faith right now and go with this feeling. I decided that it would have to become my mission to accept all of the opportunities that He laid before me as little blessings, each one a stone for my path. I would accept them with appreciation and give back by trying my best every single time. I realized that just because I'm unsure doesn't mean that God is as well. With that, I put all of my faith in him and completely changed my attitude about the audition. I made up my mind not to care so much about the destination, and simply enjoy the journey.

Once I made the decision there was a lot of work to do. It was time to come up with the best songs to sing, and to also start thinking about what parts of the song I wanted to highlight. I needed something that I genuinely enjoyed singing but that would also show my vocal range. If I was going to do this, I was determined to do it right, and after years of practicing so many songs, I knew it would be a critical selection. I even started to have fun going through all of the music that I'd accumulated over the years, to finally have a reason to choose the ones that made me the happiest. My dad asked me to make a list of the songs that I thought I would like to sing and then helped me narrow it down to the three or four that seemed to have the best potential for me to connect with. I was torn between "Joyful Joyful" and "I'll Be," two songs I knew well and really loved to sing.

It was also time to start thinking about who to tell and what to say about this whole *Idol* experiment. I've never been one to get too riled up over things, and I wanted to keep cool and not make a big deal about it. I decided not to tell any of my friends because I honestly thought that I would be back in Utah right away, and I didn't want to suffer the humiliation of letting people down. I wanted to stay as realistic as possible, and I didn't want to turn a potentially disappointing scenario into a shameful return home. It was enough that I had built up the courage to go; but to keep myself sane about it, I felt I really had to keep a low profile.

In fact, right before the auditions in San Diego, I was attending a youth conference with people from my church, which was kind of like a retreat for kids my age where we rode horses and played games— you know, all the typical camping-type stuff. To make my flight for California on time, I would have to leave the youth conference early.

And I felt really bad, because the venue of the conference was out in the middle of nowhere at a ranch in the mountains, about two hours away from the airport.

I didn't tell anyone at the retreat what my plans were, but we had to make arrangements with the conference leaders for me to get driven to the airport at a certain time. The leaders, of course, wanted to know why, considering that the drive to the airport would be such a trek. The worst part about it was that I didn't even want to leave the conference; it was such a good time, all my friends were there, and it wasn't the kind of thing that happened every weekend. It was actually a rare treat and I was having a blast. For a minute there, I was really torn about leaving, thinking about what a colossal waste of time the drive to the airport would actually be. I probably wouldn't pass the audition and I would have left the conference for no reason.

We ended up telling one of my leaders why I had to leave early. I thought it'd be okay for one person there to know what I was up to; what I didn't know was how much she liked to talk. I remember seeing her on the phone with my dad, hang up, and then walk over to where the rest of the leaders were sitting. And I could literally read her lips—A-M-E-R-I-C-A-N I-D-O-L—as she told her colleagues about my plan. To make a long story short, word spread quickly, and by the end of the trip, everyone knew. I didn't make a big deal about it, but inside I was pretty upset with this woman, because the one thing that I really wanted to avoid was a whole bunch of commotion over something that I didn't think was going to pan out anyway.

My dad and I flew to San Diego together, and just being on the airplane, I could already feel the adrenaline pumping through me. The anticipation was starting, and I started to wonder what it would be like to actually experience the process in person. I remember looking out the window of the plane and just being proud of myself for having the courage to take this risk, but also super-nervous about how it would all play out. Either way, it was going to be some kind of adventure, and from the get-go, I told myself to relax into it and try to enjoy the process, whatever it would be. I didn't have any expectations about winning and I was well aware of the fact that I would be among thousands of people who were all probably as excited and nervous as I was—and probably a lot more talented, too.

If I thought I had gone to the "School of *American Idol*" back in season one as a fan, coming back now as a competitor felt like the "University of *American Idol*." And this time, I wasn't just an innocent little boy singing in a lobby with nothing to lose. This time I was part of the game.

Once we got to San Diego, we rented a car and sped over to the general area of the auditions. We were happy to find out that we didn't really have to stay there in line all night and the next day and that we were able to just drive up and get a wristband without much of a problem. We were told they weren't even going to allow anyone to stand in line until the morning of the auditions, which was a bit of a relief. I remember when the second season auditions were going on when I was down there for *Star Search*; we drove over to the Rose Bowl and saw thousands of people with tents, sleeping bags, and fold-up chairs all just waiting until the next day's auditions. I'm glad they made it a bit easier this year. So after a few hours of rest that night, my dad dropped me off at about two a.m. so I could get what I hoped would be a good spot in line. Oh boy, I thought. This is going to be

This time I was part of the game.

nuts. There were already if not thousands at least hundreds of people lined up; everyone geared up with snacks and blankets, many of them asleep in lawn chairs, some of them singing or humming, some of them chatting the night away. Most people were just sitting around and waiting. I made friends with some of the people who were near me, and I think some of them felt badly for me because I was just this kid sitting there quietly. I would try to practice a bit to myself, and they would try to reassure me. "We heard you singing. You'll be okay. Don't worry," they said. Even though it was an audition for a competition, there was a warm sense of camaraderie in the air, which was probably just the collective energy of everyone's excitement to be there.

I was sitting near a group of people who seemed to be part of a gospel choir, which, of course, made me feel like a fish out of water. All of these big, powerful voices—and little me just sitting there wondering how the heck I was going to deliver. They would not stop singing, which at first was really cool, but after a few hours, I think everyone around them (myself included) just wanted to get some rest. At four a.m. they were still going at it, which I guess shows how determined and pumped they were for what lay ahead. I managed to sneak in an hour or so of sleep, leaning up against the wall of the stadium.

The next morning, we all had to wait in a whole other line, which is when we would get the chance to sing. Having been surrounded by gospel singers with powerful voices, I felt that maybe I should sing something in that genre to show I wasn't just a pop singer. I wanted to come across as having a soulful voice, too. I thought "Joyful, Joyful" might be a good choice, and that it could show the judges that I had some soulfulness even for a kid from Utah.

After five hours, I finally got a bit closer to the front of the line and we then found out that before we all went in, we were going to have to pose for a bunch of crowd photos. They took what seemed like forever to do the group photos of us for some reason, and I just remember feeling so tired after a night of barely any sleep. I recall wishing that I could be sitting down or even lying on a bed sleeping, and I really was worried about being able to stay awake. The whole thing was totally exhausting—and back then, I didn't realize that it was only the beginning. Thank goodness, I didn't. Otherwise I don't know if I would have been able to brace myself for everything else that was going to happen. The process felt tedious and never ending in every possible way that you could imagine, but it was also kind of cool to see so many other talented singers really going for it. It reminded me of why I was here in the first place and of how excited I used to get when the show first came on. I tried to hold on to that feeling.

The whole operation was super-professional. The producers really ran a tight ship. We were constantly reminded to be on our best behavior, and they were clear about the fact that they wouldn't tolerate any messing around. I'm not sure exactly what that meant but it made me even more nervous. As the stadium filled with over ten thousand people, we could look down on the field and see a bunch of little tents set up with two to four people sitting at each table, and we saw they were going to have some more group photos and have us sing the theme song for our year before actually starting the auditions. Finally, they started filing off the first section and lined the people up in long lines, four across. I was probably three or four sections in so we figured we had a couple of hours so I just relaxed and watched a bit. My dad was the one trying to figure out exactly what was going on and figured the best thing was to just have me warm up a little bit but not too much. I would just pace myself and get warm and focus on feeling calm. As we waited, we kept looking for people to go to the right and up the steps with their golden ticket. The rejected people who were told they didn't make it walked out to the left. After what seemed like hundreds of people going to the left, we finally saw someone running up the right side with a golden piece of paper in their hands. Then it was another long wait until we saw another one. I guess this was going to be a very difficult process and I was even more nervous now thinking that there was no way I was going to make it through here in San Diego.

It soon became our section's turn and we filed off in long lines waiting and waiting. At least I was awake now, right? They set us up in four lines, one of us from each would become a group, and in turn we would then approach the audition tables. The lady I was next to also happened to be from Utah, which was nice to see. She had long blond hair and looked really stylish, and she had a cool voice, too. She helped me relax a bit. I guess a little familiarity can go a long way when you're nervous. I was the third person to sing in my group, and by the time I got to the very front of the line my exhaustion was replaced entirely with anxiety. The guy who went before me sang the Luther Vandross version of "Superstar," which totally blew my mind. He sounded so good and I thought, Wow, that guy can be in the Top 24—easily. And just as I had that thought, I heard the judges reject him, which also blew my mind, because I really thought he had what they were looking for. I realized then that this was going to be a lot less predictable than I could have imagined, and there was no telling who the judges were going to favor and who they were going to send home on the spot. I thought, I'm toast. There's almost no point in trying.

And even though I had sung on national television many times by then, now I was totally petrified. I went up and managed to get out about ten seconds of "Joyful Joyful" before the judges abruptly stopped me. Dang, I thought. They hated it. I really thought that was it for me, and that I was about to be sent home. "David, why don't you sing something a little more youthful, something a little more . . . you?" they half asked, half instructed. I was totally unsure what they meant, since I'd kind of lost touch with my true identity as a singer over the years. I didn't even know what was "me" anymore as far as singing went. I only knew that I still loved to do it.

Luckily I had my plan B song, "I'll Be," which I had thought about singing before I saw the swarm of gospel singers. There's a lot to "I'll Be," and for some reason, I've always really felt comfortable singing it. I didn't even get to the chorus. I sang thirty seconds and that was that. I thought I'd ruined my chance, because I wasn't even able to get to the good part of the song. Anyway, I felt that "Joyful, Joyful" was really going to be the song that would let me shine, so after they shut that one down, I thought, Game over. I figured they hated my first song choice, which maybe also tainted the way they would assess me. They thanked me, asked for my name and told the next person in my group to sing. As far as I was concerned, I was done. I was actually relieved that it was over. I felt I had done my bit by showing up and following through, and now I just wanted to sneak out the back door and pretend that none of it had ever happened. I kind of felt like "There, I did it. Everyone happy?"

But just as I was turning toward the exit, one of the judges said, "No, wait. You come back here." Of course I didn't think they were talking to me—I was sure they were calling out to one of the other people in my group. I turned around and said, "Meeee?" I was just hoping that I hadn't done anything wrong! Then they all looked at me, each one with their own version of a poker face, and said, "You're going to the next round." My heart dropped, my eyes widened and my palms started to sweat. I knew there were like fifty thousand people auditioning; and only two or three hundred people were given tickets to the next round. Beyond thrilling.

When I walked out of the audition room with my golden ticket in my hand, there was applause. I saw people who had stood in line with me and they were so happy for me. They told me they knew I was going to pass. I don't know how they could have, but it was nice to feel supported—even if they were still a bunch of strangers.

I felt a swirl of emotions that included happiness, confusion and total shock. For the first time in years I had a feeling of wholeness, a sense that I was starting to reconnect the dots of who I really was, and what I really wanted to do. I felt like myself again, complete once again, doing what I loved most.

That night in the hotel, I was online chatting with Lundy, one of my friends back home. He had also been at the youth conference and had heard that I was auditioning, which kind of infuriated me, because I really didn't want to come back to Utah with my tail between my legs.

The fewer people who knew, the better. I may as well shoot this thing down early, I thought to myself, so I decided to tell him the whole story about my day at the stadium, leaving out the small detail that I'd gotten a golden ticket. I simply told him that the judges stopped me in the middle of my song—which wasn't a lie, right? In general I don't like to be deceitful, but I wanted everyone to assume that I didn't pass the audition. You can call it a case of "expectation management." I saw it as critical. That was my story, and I was going to stick to it.

When we flew back to Utah, right after we landed my father dropped me off at a friend's house, where a bunch of us were going to watch *Bill and Ted's Excellent Adventure*. Lundy was there, and of course, he couldn't help himself. "Hey, everyone, guess where David just came from!" he proudly told the whole crew. "He auditioned for *American Idol*, but he didn't make it." This was received with a lots of "awww"s from the rest of my friends, but I was thrilled. This is good, I thought. No one needs to know. Since they all felt bad for me for "not making it" they also didn't want to talk about it too much so that I wouldn't be upset. Little did they know that I was slated to head back to San Diego for the next round of auditions in September. But for the time being, school was about to start again, so I tried to keep the focus on that and not get too excited about my secret. By mid-August it was time to enroll and during that time one of my close friends, Jayme, asked me to the dance that was coming up in a few months. I really wanted to say yes to her, but I also knew that there was a tiny chance that I wouldn't be around because of *American Idol*, so I wasn't sure how to handle the whole thing without blowing my cover. Since she was a good friend, I took her aside when we were at regis-

"Meeee?" I was just hoping that I hadn't done anything wrong!

tration and told her everything. Now she and Mietra, another close buddy, were the only two friends who'd heard the news directly from me. I made them promise not to tell anyone, and even though they were so excited for me, they were both incredibly respectful and discreet about it. I was so happy that I could trust my friends, and I have to admit it was kind of nice to know that they were on board with me. In the end, I was even able to go to the dance with Jayme, because it was during one of the rare moments in the course of the *Idol* adventure when I was home.

San Diego was the first of all the cities where they held auditions, and for the next month or so, they would head to the rest of the cities to make more selections. My second audition in San Diego would be for a group of producers. For this September round of auditions, they would also start interviewing me about my life and background. My biggest concern now was that I wouldn't be interesting enough. I mean, what could I really say, that I was in the high school choir? Yippee. Big deal. I felt that I didn't have a real story to tell. And the one thing the interviewers kept telling us was to not say anything about how much we loved music, because they explained that that's what everyone said, and they wanted us to all come across as individually as possible. I was mostly at a loss for words, but I remember talking to them about running, because that's something I was doing a lot of at the time. I talked about my summer job, and I talked about how watching *Les Misérables* as a kid really got me into music. I talked about my family and growing up in Florida, but beyond that I couldn't come up with anything else that was interesting about me. I didn't even know if I should talk about *Star Search* or not, worried that it was a competing show; and besides, that was a few years ago and the second year I didn't do very well anyway. I just didn't know what to say.

For that round, I sang "I Don't Want to Miss a Thing" and managed to get to the next round, which was just two days later. Now it was time to sing for the executive producers. I chose to sing "I'll Be" again, and again they asked me to sing something else. So I went back to "I Don't Want to Miss a Thing," which had seemed to go well in the previous round. As I was singing, the executive producers stopped me. They said that I seemed to be gasping a bit for air, and that I sounded like I was slightly wheezing. I wasn't expecting anyone to pick up on that, and explained very matter-of-factly that one of my vocal cords had been paralyzed a few years back. I had put that out of my mind over the years and it just wasn't something that I was thinking about anymore. The moment I said the words "vocal paralysis," they all looked at one another. At first I thought I'd blown it by telling them, but then it became pretty clear that as producers, they were seeing a story here. I hadn't said anything about it in the interviews because it just wasn't something I dwelled on, and it obviously wasn't something that I liked to think about, especially on an audition for *American Idol*. But now these executives wanted to hear every little detail about it.

I hadn't checked my vocal cords in years, not since that first time when I was on *Star Search*. I didn't know if my condition had improved from a clinical point of view; I just knew that I felt better and wasn't suffering as much when I tried to sing for a long time. But I never really knew how long my voice was going to last. I was just kind of taking a chance. I was going with the flow. Remember, I didn't go on the audition to get onto the show; I just went to see what it would be like. I wasn't expecting it to go very far. I definitely didn't think I would make it on the show long enough to have to sing every week! I didn't know what my voice could really handle, but I told myself that if I made it this far, I should just keep testing the waters. After I explained myself to the execs, they told me that I was the best male vocal they had heard all day. I think they were as stunned by my story as I was by their reaction to it.

After passing these third and fourth rounds for the producers and executive producers, I would finally get the chance to sing for Simon, Paula and Randy. I was beyond terrified. It was one thing to sing for these guys in the lobby of the Renaissance Hotel back when I was a little boy. Now, even though I was older, I felt tiny in their presence. Each round had demanded that I face my fears not only in front of the judges but so many producers and fellow contestants. The whole exercise had been a test in emotional endurance. I always thought that each round would for sure be my last, and I definitely didn't have any far-fetched notions or fantasies about getting on the show. Also, I wasn't the most stylish guy at the time, so I didn't even know what I was supposed to look like when I went in there. I was used to wearing baggy clothes and didn't under-

My biggest concern now was that I wouldn't be interesting enough.

stand the concept of boys wearing clothes in a small size. But what did I know? Luckily, Mietra and Jayme helped me pull something together back in Utah before I left. Another friend came to the mall with us that day, and he kept asking why I needed all these new outfits. I didn't want to tell him, so I just said that I was on a mission to improve my style. Before I actually went in to sing for them, I sat around in a waiting room all day just practicing with headphones on. I was mostly trying to listen to songs that would calm me down. I chose John Mayer's "Waiting on the World to Change." At this point nothing felt real anymore. It all felt like an animated film or something, because everything that was happening was so out of the ordinary for me. I went into it thinking that all I could do was my very best, and swore to myself that I wouldn't be too hard on myself if something went wrong. Actually, I didn't expect it to work out, and everyone knows it's always a lot easier when you go into something with low expectations. This attitude had worked for me in the past, so I figured it would come in handy now. I just didn't want to set myself up for disappointment.

The audition itself happened so fast that I didn't have time to think. It all felt so surreal with the cameras and those hot lights shining directly into my eyes, completely blinding me. I knew the judges were all looking at me, but I could not see any of them. It almost felt like I was singing into a vacuum. Everything in front of me looked cloudy, like some sort of dream state, or like I was staring straight into the center of the sun. It was only when I heard Randy chime in, actually singing along with me, that it hit me again that I was actually singing for the *American Idol* judges!

"You're going to Hollywood," they said, and for the first few moments I couldn't believe it was true. I thought I was being punk'd! I was sure Simon was going to say something bad, because I even messed up the words. But instead everyone was extremely positive and seemed to be genuinely pleased with what they heard. Simon even said that it was a good song choice, and they collectively gave me three yeses, which really surprised me because I thought for sure at least one of them was going to say no. I couldn't understand it: How could they not pick up on how nervous I was? How could they not see right through me? Didn't they hear me mess up the lyrics? Apparently not, because I left that audition room with a golden ticket in my sweaty hand.

The next day, I woke up thinking, Did that really just happen? Did I really just pass the audition for Simon, Randy, and Paula? This kind of thing doesn't happen to people normally. At least not to me. I don't think I knew how to feel. Grateful, yes; but totally shocked at the fact that I had gotten this far, and terrified about continuing to compete at this level.

"Hollywood Week" was in November, which meant I would have to leave school once again. By this point, no matter how much I tried to stay quiet about my *American Idol* secret, it became useless. There were many people who, in addition to being my friends, were also big fans of the show, and they were keeping up with the audition process online. They started to notice that I was always taking

Auditioning in front of Paula, Simon, and Randy for American Idol

off mysteriously close to when the next round of auditions was taking place, so of course they started to get suspicious.

For the next month or so we were back at home preparing for Christmas and trying not to think too much about things that were out of our control with the show. I would imagine they would watch our tapes and interviews and assess us one more time before they decided who would make it to the Top 24. They told us to come back to L.A. at the end of January. It all started to feel more official, more serious. I'm sure all the contestants could feel this for what they called "The Green Mile," which was when we'd learn who they had chosen.

If you could believe it, I still didn't want to tell anyone about what was happening, maybe because I myself had a hard time believing it. It seemed that the farther along I got, the more I wanted to downplay the whole thing. I didn't want to create a frenzy among my friends, especially since I was in high school. You know how teenagers can be about things. I wanted to find a way to enjoy the process while at the same time keeping my cool.

But there was only so much "information wrangling" that I could do, because in December they aired a commercial with people who passed the first auditions, so people were completely shocked when they saw me in a TV commercial for the seventh season of *American Idol*. I got more text messages after that commercial aired than I had ever received altogether.

Around this time I was in a singing group in school with some of my friends, and we sang at church and other local events for fun. One day I was driving to a rehearsal with my friend Ashley, who was in the group and knew nothing of my recent adventures in auditioning. I heard the chime signaling I'd gotten a text message, and since I was driving, I asked Ashley to read it. It was from someone who had just seen me on the commercial, completely freaking out. Ashley read it and proceeded to freak out herself. "What!!!??? You didn't tell me!" She was out of control.

From that point on, the news started to spread and there was nothing I could do but accept it. Word was out, and I figured if I was going to be big enough to show up for the Green Mile decisions, I would have to be big enough to accept all that came with it.

To add to the stress, I had heard all the horror stories about Hollywood Week. Everyone always said it was a nightmare, loaded with pressure, tension, and all kinds of anxiety. I remember on past seasons during Hollywood Week, you would always see contestants crying and freaking out. I was sure this would be the end of the line for me.

For Hollywood Week, we would each sing two songs alone on the stage for the judges, but this time we would all watch one another perform. We had to sit in assigned seats in the theater according to the order in which we'd sing. Any contestants who were minors, such as myself, had their parents sitting in a special area designated for guardians. The show producers were running a pretty tight ship, that's for sure. We were instructed not to talk about anything that was going on, because it all had to be kept in total confidentiality, but of course there were people who would sneak around and blog or text their friends and fan Web sites with the scoop about what was happening.

Sitting to the left of me was Ramiele Malubay, which was cool because she also ended up getting to the Top 10. To my right was Amanda Overmyer, who also made it to the Top 12. She was kind of a rocker/biker girl and she really cracked me up. She was so cavalier, just sitting there reading her book. "You're a lil' sweetheart!" she said to me. I got a huge kick out of her, and she definitely made the waiting process that much more endurable.

We had been told to pick and learn one song from a list that we were given a few weeks earlier, and to figure out what key we were going to sing in. We decided at home to have a few songs ready, and even one that I could play on piano which I really didn't want to do but I finally agreed to at least learn it just in case. At first I chose "(Everything I Do) I Do it for You"; then it struck me that a lot of other people were singing it, so I thought I'd change my strategy. I had actually worked out an arrangement for it on the piano after a lot of prodding from my dad, and as I wanted something more interesting for the moment of truth, I went with "Crazy" by Gnarls Barkley and decided to play it on piano despite how nervous I was about playing while I sang. This was a whole new thing for the show, because it was the first season in which singers were allowed to play instruments, which to me instantly raised the bar. I practiced the whole night before on a little rollout keyboard that I'd brought with me. We had a brief rehearsal with the vocal coaches and piano accompanists, and most of the people singing "Crazy" were just doing it with the accompanist. A few others sang it while playing the guitar and I was the only one accompanying myself at the piano.

On the first day, which was a Tuesday, everyone was to sing what they had practiced from the list, and if you made it past that round you automatically got to skip the next round on Wednesday—they called it a "free pass." If you didn't pass, you'd get a second chance on Wednesday to sing just fifteen to twenty seconds of a song. Although I was excited about the whole idea of performing solo in front of the judges, I was so nervous about playing the piano while singing that I had to have a quick little prayer to help me remain calm. Well, it worked!! Thankfully, I was spared because I made it through on the first day when I sang "Crazy." Appropriately enough, the whole thing was beyond crazy. I remember thinking that Simon was going to say it was terrible, because just like the first time, I messed up the words and I didn't think they would tolerate that kind of sloppiness at this point in the audition process.

But instead, Simon said: "I think. . .that was incredible!" When I heard those words come out of Simon's lips, of course my heart leaped. I didn't know what to do with myself. I just stood there with sweaty palms and my heart racing probably faster than I have ever felt it race. I felt cold and hot at the same time, and my entire body started to tingle. I wasn't sure if I was hallucinating or if what had just come out of Simon's mouth was actually real. I didn't even know if what had come out of my mouth when I sang had been any good or not. But when I saw Paula, Randy and Simon all looking at me with smiles on their faces, I knew I had to say something.

"What??? . . . Oh . . ." That was my brilliant response. I couldn't believe it had gone that well; I wasn't expecting them to even like it. What I do know for sure is that when I sang that song, my heart was 100 percent into it. I guess that came across because they all said it was one of the best male vocals they had heard all day. This was an important moment for me, not just for the obvious reasons, but also because their unexpectedly positive reactions gave me the push of confidence that I would need to move any farther along. I could step up to whatever challenge was coming with the knowledge that these people liked what they heard. That was definitely enough to get me started.

Courtesy of Jenna Enns

The look on my face here says it all: happy and excited all at once

But I didn't want get too ahead of myself, and tried to just see that moment for what it was: a baby step of progress. Not toward the goal of being on the show necessarily, but for the sake of my ability to start believing in any positive feedback that I would get. I stayed on course with the decision of not telling anyone and just kept looking forward.

For the next round on Thursday, there was a giant list of songs that we could choose from. We couldn't just sing whatever we wanted because of licensing issues; we could only sing songs that were cleared by the show. I picked "Heaven" by Bryan Adams. I remember rehearsing with the musical directors, Debra Byrd and Michael Orland, which was also when we finally started singing with the band. Everything was starting to feel more official, more serious. I'm sure all the contestants could feel this professional shift in the way things were being handled, and we all tried our best to step it up. There was a very synergistic vibe in the air. Everyone was so excited, and clearly inspired by the amazing singing we were getting to hear from one another. There was so much raw talent on that stage, so many different voices and styles. It was beyond awesome.

The three days gave us the chance to start mingling, too. I remember meeting Michael Johns, and for the first time seeing David Cook perform. I also got to meet Brooke White, who was in the Top 5, and I clicked with her instantly. It was so nice to be able to make a friend with similar background and values to share this experience with. But at the end of each of those days, I came back to the hotel where we were all staying and practiced my songs or the piano. I was happy to be meeting other people but I didn't want to get too distracted.

During these days, we also had lots of interviews with more producers and executives. By now we were also being filmed, and having the camera on me was by far one of the most difficult things to get used to. I don't have to remind you of my shyness, so imagine me trying to not come across like Mr. Awkward every time we had to film an interview. I had to work really hard to keep myself together, which I did by acting like I didn't care that a camera was up in my face. Fake it until you make it, right? In time it would get easier to do, but those first few interviews were especially intimidating and worse than a total nightmare.

After I sang in the third round, Simon said he didn't like "Heaven" as much as he had liked "Crazy," but that it was still good. He seemed pleased (well, as pleased as Simon ever gets); and the rest of the judges gave positive comments, too. Once again, against everything that I thought was going to happen, I passed. I was now one of fifty people in the running to be on the show.

The Green Mile would make up an entire episode of the show, and took place in the same location as Hollywood Week. Only this time, none of us would sing. There would only be more interviews and then finally the selection announcements. We all sat in a waiting room wondering what the heck was going on. People were there with their families, so it was a pretty emotionally charged scene. There were lots of tears—both of sadness and joy. Every time someone came back after being called in, the look on his or her face would tell us what the decision had been.

> ... having the camera on me was by far one of the most difficult things to get used to.

I wish I could tell you that I remember how I felt or what the judges' exact words were when they told me that I was one of the ones selected. I had prepared myself so much to be told no that I had no idea what to do with the news that I had actually made it. The tingles came back again, and this time they were all over my face. Now I felt my heart beating in every part of me. So many thoughts ran through my brain: Would I have to leave school? Would my family really be cool with this? What would it be like to be one of the youngest people on the show?

I just wanted to sing.

When I came back out to the waiting room to tell my dad and aunt the amazing news, all I remember is that there was a camera in my face and people were screaming. It was such a crazy commotion that the details are just fuzzy to me. I'm sure we all hugged and went bonkers together for a moment, but it's really all kind of a blur.

Once the full Top 24 were announced, there was a huge celebration with us all dancing and rejoicing in the fact that we had come this far. It was a great opportunity to get to know the people who we'd be spending the next chapter of our lives with, and now it really felt like we were on the brink of a serious journey.

Even though I was in the Top 24, I still didn't think I had the slightest chance to win and just kept trying to forget the fact that I was part of a contest. You see, I didn't really want to compete—I just wanted to sing.

CAREFUL WHAT YOU WISH FOR

"If you play music with passion and love and honesty, then it will nourish your soul, heal your wounds and make your life worth living. Music is its own reward."

—STING

6

My experience on the show would be slightly different from those of the contestants who weren't minors. For one thing, my dad would be there with me as my legal guardian while the show was putting us up, and I would also have to go to three hours of school every day.

I imagined that I'd be back in school in no time and felt that I should do everything in my power to stay caught up. I didn't even say good-bye to anyone at school that January because I was sure I'd be seeing them all again real soon.

But my high school principal said that even though everyone at school was really excited for me, I had to withdraw because my district had very particular rules about attendance. I'm sure many kids would have been thrilled to withdraw from high school, but I felt terrible about it. I've always taken school and grades very seriously, and having to make this choice was bigger and scarier than deciding to quit my summer job. This was high school we were talking about. It was scary enough to be part of the competition to begin with; but the prospect of failing in that context and failing school just seemed like too dark a place to end up. Other young contestants who had been on the show were able to get work sent to them. But my school district was more strict, and this just wasn't an option for me. They wouldn't make an exception. I was told that I wouldn't be able to finish my junior year—at least not with the rest of my class. I tried to take online classes, like other minors had in previous seasons, but I just couldn't concentrate. It wasn't for me.

All of the kids under eighteen were assigned a studio teacher once we were in the Top 24 and had begun working on the live shows. My teacher and I would work together for a few hours each day, and luckily during the Top 24, there were other minors who were in the same boat as me, so at least in the beginning I wasn't alone. I became really close to them because we had similar schedules, which was a nice way to start out the season; but at the same time it made it that much more sad for me to see them go when they did. Even when I went to regular school, it had taken a lot of effort for me to get good grades; now, as I juggled the competition with trying to be a student, it sometimes felt impossible. I couldn't even focus, let alone absorb a lot of what was being taught to me. Often, my mind was just somewhere else.

And even though I had the studio teacher, and as excited as I was about the *Idol* experience, the reality that I had to officially withdraw from high school definitely felt like a small crisis. You have to understand that one of the reasons grades have always been really important to me is that as much as I loved music and hoped I could have a future in music, I never counted on music to work out for me as a life path. I just always thought I'd need some kind of plan B. Good grades would

Here is a happy me around the age of about three years old.

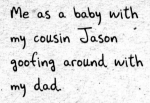

Me as a baby with my cousin Jason goofing around with my dad.

Here we are at Universal Studios.

I must be about fifteen or sixteen in this one. I look calm. That's always good!

In snowy Utah. I was never the biggest fan of the cold.

Rollerblading has always made me feel free. I used to love it as a little kid

Here we are in our school uniforms.

Courtesy of the author

Happy Birthday Daddy!

Courtesy of the author

One time we were gone on a summer trip that my dad couldn't come to because of work. It was his birthday while we were away, so we took a group picture to let him know we were thinking of him.

Courtesy of the author

Courtesy of the author

I was lucky enough to get to sing a solo at the baptism.

We're singing at a baptism in this one.

Stadium shows really give you an adrenaline rush!

2005.03.11 16:16

Practicing my piano. Always key.

My sister Jazzy standing next to me as I sign an autograph. Signing autographs has always been strange but flattering!

Here I am rehearsing with Dolly Parton when I sang "Smokey Mountain Memories" on American Idol.

I couldn't believe I was standing and singing like three feet away from Mariah!

Salt Lake City gave me my own street sign. Ha ha.

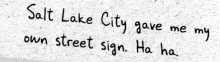

Coming home to Murray, Utah, was one of the coolest things ever.

SALT LAKE COUNTY
SALT LAKE COUNTY
IDOL

ARCHULETA AVE

TODAY

ROCKEFELLER PLAZA

NO
6 AVE

David Cook and I at the Today show.

This is a Clarkston, Michigan, show in the summer of 2009 with Demi Lovato.

Another pic from Clarkston, Michigan, with Demi Lovato. This was a fun show because it's one of the few amphitheater shows I've gotten to do.

One World. One Love. One David.

Here I am with some awesome fans in Kuala Lumpur, Malaysia.

I'm superamped at this concert in Houston, Texas.

I love my fans!

This shot was taken by a fan during a tour. Glad I was smiling!

Courtesy of Emily Harmon

Courtesy of Emily Harmon

Courtesy of Jennifer Uriegas

Happy to be meeting all the fans. It was really fun seeing what people had to say, and some of them had some pretty interesting gifts to give too!

This is another candid shot taken by a fan during a tour.

Here I am on a TV show in the Philippines.

I'm feeling the vibe at this concert in Hershey, Pennsylvania.

I love being able to play the piano while I sing. It can really add to a song and the show.

I love singing Christmas songs. It's always uplifting.

Courtesy of Chelsea Stannard

Nothing like holiday
spirit to keep the
inspiration flowing.

Courtesy of Kim Meade

Singing for a roomful
of people somehow
feels like a blessing.

Thinking about what the song is about before it starts.

Here I am with the one and only Lady Gaga, at Madison Square Garden.

At my first-ever CD signing at the Virgin Megastore in Times Square in New York City!

When it comes down to it, it's all about feeling a connection to the song.

give me the chance to make solid choices about college and could open the door to having a worthwhile career. The idea of risking this almost felt like a mistake. But I guess that was how I learned that sometimes you have to take a risk when there's an opportunity right under your nose. No matter how hard things seemed to get, it also began to get clearer and clearer that there would be no turning back. Once you're in the show, you're in the show, and I wasn't about to walk away from that. Quitting would have equaled failure; so giving up was never an option, the same way it hadn't been an option to give up at the Utah talent show a few years back.

At some point, it just hit me that music should be my focus, no matter how things turned out. Yes, school was important, and yes, I was taking a major risk, but I tried to reach back to that moment I had knelt by my bed and talked to God and remember that I was here for a reason. I started working on songs twenty-four hours a day, seven days a week (except for the three hours a day of school and a little sleep once in a while). On *American Idol*, that wasn't too shabby. I would say to myself, "David, remember that this is a good thing—the opportunity may have come a bit sooner than expected, but here it is nonetheless. Take it. Run with it. This is my dream coming true." My parents were, of course, delighted and excited, but they didn't want to get ahead of themselves either, and tried to follow my lead on staying calm. They would be a tremendous support system for me, and I know I wouldn't have been able to get through some of the hardest moments without my dad's on-site wisdom and support, and the comforting sound of my mom's voice on the phone.

My poor brother and sisters were really the ones who had to put up with the most, because by now everyone at school knew that "David Archuleta" was their brother. They were constantly approached as "David's brother or sister" and sort of lost their own identities, which made it a rough time for them. They just wanted to be themselves and have their space. Nothing in their lives had really changed; yet they

> **the reality that I had to officially withdraw from high school definitely felt like a small crisis.**

were being hit with the *Idol* mania on a daily basis just because they were my family. They wanted privacy, and out of nowhere they were tossed into the madness with me. Only I got to live tucked away in L.A., but they had the burden of showing up at school every day to face everyone's comments. I mean, how many times in one day can a person hear "You're David's brother?" I felt bad for them but knew they would be fine once *Idol* mania died down.

No amount of mental preparation could have possibly primed me for the fact that for the next five months, I would be living in L.A. to learn, rehearse and ultimately sing a total of nineteen songs live on *American Idol* alongside a bunch of older (and way more experienced) singers, the whole time camped out in an apartment with my father and doing all my schoolwork with a studio teacher, Wendy, instead of actually going to high school. As exciting as it all was, my life felt like it was someone else's. In my mind's eye, I would look down at myself like a fly on the wall of my own experience; and each time I had to really shake myself to realize that it was all actually happening to me.

Think about it: From the moment I was announced as one of the Top 24, I went from being just David to David-Archuleta-on-*American-Idol*. It felt like such a massive responsibility. All of a sudden people expected me not only to perform, but also to continually outdo myself. Not only would I be up against so many other amazing talents, but also I had to surpass the bar that I would set for myself each week. We were now in a competition that included individual progress as one of the key variables to win. Even though I was stoked about being on the show, I also thought that I was the worst person there. Every week, I assumed that I was going to be the next one sent home. I honestly didn't think there was anything special about me. Those few months would be full of equal parts joy and stress, and there were many moments when I didn't know if I would be able to handle another minute. Keep in mind that overnight I went from being a regular high school kid (a position I worked hard to get after being a *Star Search* kid) to being on the biggest show on TV. Remember that I was for the most part shy and quiet, and all of this new exposure was kind of mortifying. From one day to the next, I had thrown myself into the lion's den, exposing myself to the world, setting myself up for who knows what kind of disasters. The very thought of being on live television every week was incredibly stressful for all of us. No one (except for Jason Castro!) was ever relaxed. I know I constantly had that tense feeling in my shoulders. I'm not saying it wasn't fun; but it was a lot of work and every day felt like a series of hurdles to get past with next to no time. But at one point I told myself that no matter how nerve-racking the whole thing was, it would be more productive to enjoy it, rather than suffer in anxiety the whole time.

Every week I had to pick the right song, work on its arrangement, practice, and try to keep up with studio school as much as possible. Throughout all of those months, it seemed like we oftentimes didn't even have enough time to prepare for that week's music, and the various random tasks that got added to our already crazy schedules made it very difficult to juggle everything. Every night we would receive a text message giving us the next day's itinerary. Most days started as early as five or six in the morning, and wouldn't end until ten or eleven at night. I would typically wake up, rehearse, shower and then leave for the studio, where I would spend a few hours in school. Sundays usually meant a full day of shooting music videos, from morning to night. On top of rehearsing and filming the video, which usually went late into the evening, we would find a CD under our door upon arriving home that we had to rehearse for our iTunes recording session the next morning. Again, because I would have school, I usually had to go first which means I had very little time to rehearse and prepare my song. After recording on Monday, I would rehearse my song with the band and do a rough sound check. That was my chance to tell the band what I wanted the song to sound like, which could be really stressful due to there being only one hour to try to make sure everything was just right. It was a challenge for me to know how to explain everything I was hoping to be in the song in the proper music language so the band could understand what I meant, but it was a good opportunity for me to learn a lot about communicating on a musical and verbal level. After that rehearsal, most people got to take a load off and have a rest, but of course I'd still have to go back to school.

On non-show days, mixed in with a few hours with my studio teacher, I would get pulled out to rehearse my song again with the show's musical directors. Some days we also had photo shoots, or promotional appearances, or had to film more interviews for the show. We were always doing something.

On Tuesdays, the morning of the show, we would work with the production crew to rehearse onstage for the actual performance. There were always tons of cameras around the singers onstage, and the musical directors and stage manager would also give us tips on where to look, and how to angle our bodies. Everyone always had something to say—that's for sure.

Tuesdays were also when we would rehearse the group numbers that we'd perform on the Wednesday results shows, which was the last thing anyone ever wanted to do. We had enough on our own plates without also having to think about group numbers with the people we were competing against. But once Tuesday afternoons were over and done with, I would feel a huge sense of relief. By then, the song was chosen, arranged, rehearsed, and that was it. There was nothing more you could do at that point but wait for the live show to start, and then when it's your turn to give it your best shot and go for it! After the show, we would usually go over to a restaurant with our family who was usually there for the live show or whatever friends might be there for a bite to eat and to try to relax a little bit. It was the closest thing to down time we had the entire week.

That quick breath of relief was short-lived, though, because Wednesday was just as packed as every other day, with dress rehearsals for the results show, especially the dreaded group numbers. In addition to those rehearsals, interviews and, in my case, school, some weeks you also had to start thinking about your song for the following week. On Wednesday or Thursday morning, we'd be given the list of songs to choose from, and by a certain time they would give us, we would have to pick three possibilities off the list. And we had to be sure about them, because once we submitted our choices, we were committed to performing one of the three. I didn't even know a lot of the songs, sometimes I had to sacrifice school time to meet the deadlines they gave us and research various renditions so I could figure out what my own take would be. Thankfully, Wendy was very understanding and would let me take whatever time I needed to meet my deadlines. She understood that my main reason to be there was to do as well as I could each week and she made sure she gave me as much flexibility as possible to keep up with everything.

On the Wednesday show, someone would get voted off, of course, and that person would have to fly out the next morning to do a week of press. So after the show, we always had a farewell dinner as a group. It was bittersweet, because even though it was nice to spend time together, the good-bye factor made it kind of tough. It was really fun though because we actually did a roast of the person who was leaving and they had a chance to say something about all of us too so it was sad but very fun and memorable. If you're going to get voted off, at least this helped soften the blow quite a bit.

Sometime between Thursday and Sunday, we'd go shopping for outfits for the upcoming week. There was a stylist who would help us, but we mostly were able to choose what we felt comfortable in. By this point in the week, we would also have narrowed down our list of three songs to one, and spent a lot of time working on the arrangement and rehearsing. If you couldn't decide which of the three songs you wanted to do, the musical directors would help you figure out the best choice. Even then sometimes you'd pick a song only to find out that you couldn't sing it after all (whether it wasn't right for your pitch or simply a bad song choice to begin with), so you'd have to go back to the drawing board and pick another one.

Even with the nightly text message, you never knew exactly how each day would play out. You had to be ready for anything, and the one thing you knew for sure was that your life was completely dedicated to the show. It didn't matter what the schedule was, you had to do whatever they said and be wherever they wanted you. There was not much wiggle room for anything, and because we were all committed, we just played along and did what we were told.

A lot of the time while I was at "school," my dad would start working on the arrangements; then we'd talk about them and figure out which song had the best potential. I'd learn them, and together we'd try to figure out how to make the performances interesting. The challenge each week was to find ways to build unique and special moments into each song. We would ask ourselves, "Are there any obvious places we can build in a special moment at a certain point in the song? Is there something that we should change?" We were always on the hunt for those moments. I knew that I needed to do something a little bit different to each song, even if that meant just holding a note out a tiny bit longer or changing the melody slightly. I remembered his insights from when I was younger, and knew that he was right now more than ever. I had to make the music somehow unique if I wanted to stand out. Even though I would always rehearse, my mission for each show was to sound spontaneous and in the moment. I was lucky to have my

CHORDS OF STRENGTH

father by my side because our musical intuition is very similar, which I think made it easy to speak the same language when it came to working on the arrangements.

Looking back, I think I felt the freest at the beginning of the competition because at that point even if people did have expectations of me, they couldn't have been that high. Ironically, the moment the positive feedback started is when the fear of failure really set in, because I knew that people would always want me to do better than the last time. For Seventies Week on the second live show, I sang "Imagine," and even though everyone loved it, I felt that I sort of set myself up for disaster. I didn't even know what I had done to receive such a good response, so I didn't think there was a way for me to be able to repeat it, never mind outdo it. Now everyone had this image of me that I would have to uphold. After "Imagine," no one even remembered that I had sung "Shop Around" the first week, which was a fun, up-tempo song that is generally a crowd-pleaser. But each week was a completely unique experience, sixties, seventies, eighties, Beatles, whatever style or genre we were assigned, it was always a fun challenge to find a song from the list that I felt I could make my own. Some weeks were easier than others, but in the end, each one had some interesting lesson to impart.

Still, though, there was always some kind of curveball. For example, two days after I sang my first rendition of "Imagine" during the second week, I felt like I was getting hit with another cold and my voice just quit working. I just couldn't get anything out. It was really stressful, because I knew I wouldn't be able to deliver without full use of my voice. I was pretty sure I was simply coming down with something, but to be safe I consulted Dr. Nassir, the same specialist who had given me the vocal paralysis diagnosis years back when I was on *Star Search*. He was happy to help like always, and he said he couldn't believe that I was still able to sing. After scoping my throat again, he pulled up the pics of my cords from now and before when he originally scoped them. They looked totally different from each other, which was really scary. He explained that I still had a paralyzed vocal cord, but that my cords had found a way to work around the condition because by some miracle, they were vibrating despite what medically wasn't supposed to be able to happen. Despite this physical abnormality, I was able to get the songs out. The one vocal cord, it seemed, had actually grown up over and around the weak one in order to adjust for the other one not working. So in the end, it really was just a winter cold or something this time; and I'm pretty sure lack of sleep didn't help either. It was only the beginning and I was already feeling worn out. But I got through it by resting my voice whenever I wasn't rehearsing and just had faith that whatever was meant to be would be.

So that week was Eighties Week, and I decided to sing "Another Day in Paradise." It wasn't the strongest song for me, but I kind of felt I needed to play it a little safe with my voice feeling so weak. This was also an opportunity to play the piano, even though I didn't have a lot of time to practice because I was originally going to sing "Every Breath You Take" and changed my mind at the last moment. I started to feel that the lyrics to "Every Breath" were a little too . . . um . . . stalkerish. My friends actually used to call it the stalker song, so I wanted to make sure that my song choices would reflect my character and values as genuinely as possible, and felt that "Another Day in Paradise" was more attuned to who I am. That song isn't necessarily a "singer's song" and is not really upbeat or happy, but it's about real life and serious issues, such as poverty and the idea of not taking anyone for granted. Playing the piano was an opportunity to also show that I was a rounded performer, someone who could connect to every part of the song, not just hold a note or handle a long vibrato. It was so gratifying to be able to play the piano live in front of so many people after years of feeling like I wasn't any good. I was starting to understand the piano as an extension of my performance, a tool that could help me relay the emotion of a song, and another incredible way for me to express myself musically. I was finally starting to feel more confident with myself as a musical person.

But it certainly wasn't easy. Every time I sang, I expected to get ripped apart by Simon. It became a running joke with some of my fellow contestants, who were all well aware of my self-image issues. But as I saw it, this self-doubt was a way of being honest with myself, of keeping myself in check. In fact, I didn't see it as a bad thing. I was harder on myself than the judges ever were. I thought I'd be lucky if there was one person out there watching me on TV who might be affected in some tiny way by my singing. If I could accomplish only that, I've succeeded. But I didn't think I was really what the judges were looking for. I thought they were looking for "real" singers. Actually, I thought they were looking for stars. And that wasn't me.

Courtesy of Lindsay Farnworth

Playing piano has brought me to a whole new level of musicianship

Anytime I got positive feedback from the judges I was surprised. I had a hard time understanding what they heard in me. I thought, Why are they so impressed? I didn't get it. And instead of being happy when I did receive positive feedback, I would see it as some kind of burden: Now they have even more expectations of me, I would think, and next week they're going to be disappointed if I don't deliver. I'd get worried thinking that people would want whatever happened before to happen again and, honestly, a lot of the time I didn't even know what had happened in the first place! I didn't have a formula, and I didn't have a plan I could duplicate each week. I'd just hope I had picked a good song that America and the judges would like, go up there, open my mouth and hope for the best.

On certain occasions, it seemed that maybe the judges were actually feeling what I felt when I sang, and that maybe their positive reactions were a reflection of those emotions. I started to think about what it was that was giving me the courage to get up there each time, curious about how someone as naturally introverted as myself could make it through a grueling process such as this one. The answer that came to me was a lot simpler than I'd imagined: From the moment I'd start to sing (onstage or in a rehearsal), I would just allow myself to flow. I'd almost forget where I was. Whatever I was thinking about before would disappear and in its place would come only thoughts about the song. This let me pour my heart out into each song and connect to its feeling, whether I had gone through something like that or not. Thankfully, I've always been emotionally affected by music, and I think it's what has always helped me tap into the feeling that would guide each song. The music itself would always lead the way for me, its power stamping out the fear and killing the doubt. The music was the thing that saved me each time. After a while it started to feel like living in some sort of protected bubble. Everything was taken care of for us; we didn't have to decide what to do each day, much less cook, clean or do laundry, so all we had to focus on was singing our best. We weren't supposed to go out by ourselves because we needed security with us at all times. When we had to go somewhere, we would move in specially designated vans, and for the most part we traveled together everywhere we went. The other contestants were my family for half a year. We pretty much spent all of our time together, forever sitting in the same rooms together waiting for things to happen. The only people we could relate to were one another, and the only zone of comfort we knew was this new little world that we had created together.

I spent all of my time between my hotel, the room where I studied and the studio. That's it. I got so pale because I never saw sun. I started to forget what "normal life" felt like, and sometimes even got scared that I wouldn't know how to readapt when it was time to go back. I became very close with my studio teacher because she was one of the only people (other than my fellow competitors and my dad) I saw regularly. She became an all-purpose friend and counselor—teaching, supporting and listening to me. She was totally objective and had no agenda other than my well-being. I made a concerted effort to stay off the Internet as much as possible, because the people from *Idol* recommended it, and I didn't feel it was important to know what people were thinking about me. I knew how the show worked, and having been an eager fan of it myself, I knew the Web was teeming with chatter about this or that singer. I was afraid of what I would see. I honestly didn't want to know what people thought of us. I knew that if I looked, I could easily run the risk of getting upset about it, which would only make me go backward emotionally. I had to stay focused on staying positive. I did that by staying close to God and to my beliefs. But trying to be a normal teenager definitely started to feel a bit surreal. The closer we got to the finals, the more text messages I started to receive from the most random people in the world. Messages from people who I had seen my whole life but who never even noticed that I existed before they saw me on TV. My phone was always flickering and ringing to the point that I just had to ignore it. I was overwhelmed with everything else going on; the last thing I could think of was how to explain my new reputation to friends (and strangers!) whom I hadn't even told I would be here to begin with.

I knew that all of the messages were coming from a good place and more than anything people just wanted to show love and support, but honestly, it was too much, and too fast for me to feel comfortable with it. The entire framework of my social life changed radically in a matter of weeks. That just felt weird. As we got further into it, the only people I could really relate to were the people in the competition, because they knew exactly what I was going through. We were all going through it together: the self-doubt, the self-image issues, and the fear of never really knowing if you're good enough to keep going. For five months, these were the kinds of things that we woke up thinking about, and also the feelings that we'd inevitably go to bed thinking about. Once we made it to the Top 12, we moved out of the hotel and into an apartment. Our roommate for the first couple of weeks was Chikezie who was an all around great guy! My dad and I had to share a room at first, but after Chikezie was voted off in week 10, we each were able to have our own room, which was good for us both to have at least one spot where we could have some privacy.

Getting into the Top 12 was a big milestone, and I began to feel the stress of the quickly progressing season. That week was the most difficult one of the whole season because of everything that had to happen: photo shoots, interviews, iTunes versions of our songs, arrangements that turned out different from we had expected, the Ford commercials, school, rehearsals. I felt like I was completely overwhelmed. Plus all of the other minor kids were now gone so it was just me in school, no one else to share that with. We had helped support one another for those first few weeks so it was difficult when I was the last one there.

As a result of all the hectic events of that week, a new stage, me going last and having to remember to walk downstairs while I was singing, in

Jeffrey Mayer / WireImage / Getty Images

The Top 12!

a moment of panic, I completely forgot the words to "We Can Work It Out." Nightmare City! But you know what? I totally surprised myself and didn't get upset. Instead, I thought, Okay, David, what's done is done. Maybe you can learn something from this. Sometimes a little bump like this makes you stronger. I was actually proud of myself for being able to take the criticism, including Simon calling it "a mess." This was after the previous week when he'd said my performance was "a little boring." Given how insecure I was, you might think this would have torn me apart. But I think because of my self-doubt, I was able to stay open to whatever the judges had to say. I never took their comments personally and always tried to look for the helpful lesson in their critique. Their criticism didn't bother me at all. Instead, it motivated me to do better because it gave me a point of reference. I was thankful for the honesty of such an experienced group of people after so many years of hearing from friends and family that I "had talent." I was hungry to hear the advice of someone who would be willing to go deeper with me; and the *Idol* judges always came through that way. I wasn't there for pats on the back—I was there to evolve. It gave the whole experience professionalism and kept the standards of the music high.

But I was living a funny little paradox: On the one hand, I was part of a serious competition, which we realistically know implies "winning" as an objective. But on the other hand, I also knew that my own motivation had absolutely nothing to do with winning. I was there because I felt deeply that I had been handed a blessing, and to ignore that blessing would be wrong. The longer I stayed in the competition, the stronger this feeling got, and I accepted the idea that I was actually supposed to be there. I kept telling myself, "If I am still here, there must be a good reason, even if it's a reason that I can't clearly understand." But I constantly found myself trying to come to terms with the whole "pressure to win" versus enjoying the experience itself. Because for me, it was just that—an experience—a moment in my life that I'd always be able to look back on with pride, knowing that I gave it my all and worked as hard as I could.

Each time I found myself second-guessing myself or questioning my singing, I would tell myself to work that much harder. It was on me to show the judges and fans just how much I love music, to show them how songs could be magical and reach out and make people feel certain sensations and inspirations. Every day I reminded myself that this was my goal, and at each moment of the contest, I would try to look for little ways to make myself stand out more and more. Not so that I could win—but so that I could fully express my passion for music. Around this time, we also participated in a charity event called *Idol* Gives Back, which was a whole other show on top of everything else that we were doing. Everything else that normally went on continued as usual, but we had this extra show to also think about, which was so much more work. It was for a good cause, so we were happy to do it, but it was an insane week. It included appearances by people like Gloria Estefan, Mariah Carey, Sarah Silverman, Reese Witherspoon, Annie Lennox, Alicia Keys, Celine Dion, Snoop Dogg, Bono, and Fergie, to name a few. So despite the extra workload, we were all pretty thrilled to be able to participate. But there were many other things about being there that were not so easy to handle. Here's an incident that always comes to mind: On the results show of Top 7 week, we were split into two groups. In one group they put Syesha Mercado, Brooke White, and Kristy Lee Cook. The other group was Carly Smithson, David Cook, and Jason Castro. The producers decided it would be interesting to announce that I was safe and ask me which group I thought I belonged to. I have to admit, this didn't sit well with me. I hated the idea of having to pick groups, so I protested by not going to either side; instead, I sat down right in the middle of the stage, which people may have thought was cute and all, but it was really just my way of doing what I thought was right. Everyone seemed to think it was funny, but the honest truth is that I wasn't about to try to make a choice between my fellow *Idol* family. Paula was even signaling with her hand for me to sit down, so I thought I did the right thing and felt weird that they would put me in that position.

trying to be a normal teenager definitely started to feel a bit surreal.

You'd think that by this point I would have become a lot more confident and carefree onstage, but truthfully, the closer we got to the end, the less sure of myself I felt. There was so much emotion surrounding these last few shows that between the crazy schedules and the levels of hysteria in the air, many times I didn't know how I could possibly juggle it all.

The whole fame thing was tricky, too. Remember, I was in a bubble for five months straight, pretty much living in the apartment and at the FOX studio, where my life was all about arranging, rehearsing, school and everything *Idol*. So you can imagine how weird it was to fly back home to Utah during Top 3 week, only to see that the entire city had come out to greet me like one gigantic family waiting for a long-lost son. I figured I had "fans," since I kept getting voted through, but it seemed more theoretical than anything. Seeing the crowds in person, I was blown away. Words honestly can't even begin to describe how grateful and flattered I felt at the citywide welcome that I received. There was a huge celebration and swarms of people, total strangers really, who'd made a special effort to show their support. I couldn't believe how many people came out to see me, how much they appreciated what I was doing, and how happy they were for me. I could really see the pride in their eyes. I had left Utah as a scared kid with a bundle of nerves and no real sense of direction, and now here I was back home to what felt like total jubilation! I didn't know how to wrap my head around it, let alone how to respond to the crowds. I tried to be sweet and positive and to always show my gratitude for everyone's love and support. But because I'm a total introvert, it was a lot more challenging than people might think.

I could see now that my journey was as exciting to the fans as it was for me, and that even through some of my worst moments of insecurity, they had not once turned their backs on me. My fans were not simply fans; but instead a group of people who, for some reason or another, decided to unconditionally believe in me.

I soon discovered that these fans were calling themselves "Archies" or "Arch Angels," which struck me as incredibly funny, but also sweet. The fact that they had gone so far as to call themselves anything at all was flattering. Their enthusiasm for my singing would feed me with a new brand of confidence, and I can safely say that their appreciation for what I was doing is what kept me working so hard.

Of course, it was great to see the rest of my family and although the first night home I had to stay in a hotel in my own hometown, I did get to spend a few hours at home with them in between the events of the day. A lot of my relatives and friends showed up at home as well and they all showed how incredibly proud of me they were. Just the chance to be home and reconnect with everyone felt amazing. After the nonstop craziness of being on the show, it was so nice to just know I was there with my little sisters with their drawing and anime obsessions, Claudia always just being there for me and my brother just being his usual "cool" self. After being pretty much quarantined for so long under the pressure that comes with the show, I was so thankful for the time at home with the people that I loved most. It was truly a breath of fresh air. I realized how much I missed the little things in life, like waking up to have breakfast with my family, or flipping on the TV and watching some program with my sisters for some mindless entertainment, or just going out in the yard and watching the leaves move in the wind. Every day in Los Angeles was completely nuts, so the peace of being home was, as they say, just what the doctor ordered—especially now that we were really coming down to the wire.

During that Utah visit, a Mississippi woman gave me a hundred-page book she had made for me. On the cover it said, "David Is My Hero," and inside were all kinds of comments and stories from fans who had been moved by my performances. I couldn't believe that someone would take the time to put something like this together, with so much care and such attention to detail. Some celebrities might be put off by this kind of thing, maybe seeing it as a bit over-the-top. To me, however, it was a gesture of total sweetness, pure love and support. I was grateful that someone would spend even three seconds thinking about (never mind archiving) my accomplishments. I began to understand that I was somehow sharing my newfound recognition with the people who were most affected by my singing, which to me made perfect sense. It was clear that I sang for them just as much as I sang for myself, so it was fitting that we were now sharing it all together.

Life had changed so drastically since I'd left, and sometimes it felt impossible to digest it all. Things were moving so quickly and unexpectedly all the time, there was hardly ever any time to think. Even though winning wasn't my primary measurement to determine my success on the show, I totally realized it was such a great privilege to have come this far, that whether I won or not, I needed to treat the whole experience with total respect and give my absolute best effort. Otherwise, what would be the point, right? Sleep had become scarce and I was exhausted all the time. There was no denying the level of expectations and there was no hiding from the fact there were people who really wanted me to win and those that didn't. While it was super-exciting, I also felt vulnerable and misunderstood some of the time, especially when I started hearing that people and the press were spreading false rumors about me and my family and I had to fight very hard with myself to not let those things bug me. I'd remind myself to stay positive even when it seemed like my life was so overwhelming. On the one hand, I wanted to just be a normal kid, but now that I had gotten to this level of the competition, I knew that I owed it to myself, and those that were supporting me to see it through with all I could muster. I would constantly give myself little pep talks so that I would remember my original motivation and intentions, and when I didn't feel my performance was as good as it could have been after a show or started to feel nervous about how I sounded, I'd simply try to remember the better shows when I had felt on point. I would just try to redirect any negative energy that came up into trying to stay hopeful and optimistic.

The break in Utah was much needed—even though it wasn't much of a break with all the commotion. But taking that time off before returning to L.A. gave me a chance to think about the experience of being on the show, and to also start reflecting on some of the things I had learned. I started noticing some really neat changes in myself as a singer. For example, I found myself starting to think more deeply about the words that I was singing. This was kind of a new thing for me; because I started singing so young, I usually just connected with the melody and the emotion of the song and kind of took the lyrics for granted. A lot of the time I had sung without even knowing what I was singing about. Now, though, I began to really evaluate what the words meant more and more, which greatly helped me connect my own emotions with the sentiment of the song. I knew that the competition was way bigger than just being able to hold notes and carry a tune. It was about learning how to interpret those lyrics according to my personality and the ability to transmit real feelings.

One of the most memorable examples was when I chose to sing John Lennon's "Imagine" as a reprise for the finale. As I had sung it before during Top 20 week, I decided to choose it again because it was more than just a song selection for me; it was my way of communicating some of my most personal feelings. The lyrics to that song express a lot of what I care about, and reflect a sense of positivity although some people interpret it as an antiwar and/or antireligion song. To me, it is about letting go of all the negative things in the world and focusing on the positive, which is a pretty basic message, but one that has deep meaning to how I try to guide my own life. Singing that song brought me into a mental space of total peace and tranquillity, a feeling that I could almost see hovering above the crowd that was watching and listening. Both times that I sang that song, I could actually feel its impact; it was another one of those moments that affirmed the magical quality of music and the power that it has to completely penetrate a person's mind and spirit. I sang two other songs for the finale, but it was "Imagine" that crystallized the whole *Idol* experience for me. It was exactly what my love for singing is all about.

The reaction of the audience that night told me one thing: They felt what I felt. I would even go as far as saying that it was a life-changing moment for me, because it confirmed what I had always intuitively felt

TOP 5 SONGS I'VE COVERED

▶ **"Imagine"** by John Lennon because it's such a universally powerful song. It affects people in a way that is almost beyond words. It is perfect music straight from the heart, music about coming together and positivity. It was a life-changing song for me, not only in the way I saw things, but also in the way it would affect my career.

▶ **"Angels"** by Robbie Williams because it was such a big song, and I thought I could really throw myself into it and go for it.

▶ **"And I'm Telling You I'm Not Going"** from the musical *Dreamgirls* because it was the song that taught me what soul was, and how to sing with soul. Tamyra Gray sang it in the semifinals of the first season of *American Idol*, and I couldn't stop watching her or singing that song for years. In fact, it was the only song I sang for a long time. It taught me that I could go from opera boy to Motown cat.

▶ **"God Bless America"** because of the love in that song. I learned it around the time of September 11, 2001, so it resonated with me powerfully. Being able to sing that for other people was also really special, especially when I sang for a group of firemen and their families who had lost loved ones in New York. It was such a touching moment that I was honored to be a part of.

▶ **"Castle on a Cloud"** from the musical *Les Misérables* because it was the first song to ever really strike me, and though I was only five I remember it vividly.

about the power of music. I thought, I'm just this seventeen-year-old kid from Utah, but with two minutes of a song I truly felt something almost electric in the air that touched me and seemed to touch those who were listening. I felt it, and it seemed like the judges felt it and the audience as well—a collective experience of emotion, nostalgia, tenderness, hope and who knows what other feelings that were swirling around in the air that night. I was amazed at how intensely emotional I felt the whole time I was singing, and even more surprised by the way it seemed to affect others. It was like a pure spiritual connection and I'm sure that I'll always look back on the two performances of that song as some of my most special and profound musical experiences.

I think the energy was so intense that night because the reality was sinking in that the season was almost over. I had dedicated the last six months to this show, and now it was all going to finally be over. It was crazy to think that we were at the end. What was going to happen next?

I found myself starting to think more deeply about the words that I was singing

Along with the feeling of uncertainty, and even a bit of nostalgia, I can't deny that there was also a deep sense of relief. I thought to myself, *There's nothing more I can do*. At this point I definitely had a strong feeling of accomplishment and was kind of ready for the "competition side of things" to be over; no more being compared and judged every single day of my life. David Cook, the other finalist, was also tired of it. It's like everyone in the country cared about who was going to win except for us. We were just there to do music.

AMERICAN IDOL SONGS

TELEVISED AUDITION
"Waiting on the World to Change" by John Mayer

HOLLYWOOD WEEK
DAY 1
"Crazy" by Gnarls Barkley (which was never aired due to licensing issues)
DAY 4
"Heaven" by Bryan Adams

TOP 24 (TOP 12 GUYS)
"Shop Around" by Smokey Robinson and the Miracles. Performed sixth on February 19, 2008.

TOP 20 (TOP 10 GUYS)
"Imagine" by John Lennon. Performed last on February 26, 2008.

TOP 16 (TOP 8 GUYS)
"Another Day in Paradise" by Phil Collins. Performed second on March 4, 2008.

TOP 12
"We Can Work It Out" by the Beatles. Performed last on March 11, 2008.

TOP 11
"The Long and Winding Road" by the Beatles. Performed third on March 18, 2008.

TOP 10
"You're the Voice" by John Farnham. Performed eighth on March 25, 2008.

TOP 9

"Smoky Mountain Memories" by Dolly Parton. Performed third on April 1, 2008.

TOP 8

"Angels" by Robbie Williams. Performed seventh on April 8, 2008.

TOP 7

"When You Believe" by Mariah Carey and Whitney Houston. Performed first on April 15, 2008.

TOP 6

"Think of Me" by Andrew Lloyd Webber. Performed fourth on April 22, 2008.

TOP 5

"Sweet Caroline" and "America" by Neil Diamond. Performed fourth on April 29, 2008.

TOP 4

"Stand By Me" by Ben E. King and "Love Me Tender" by Elvis Presley. Performed last on May 6, 2008.

TOP 3

"And So It Goes" by Billy Joel, "With You" by Chris Brown, and "Longer" by Dan Fogelberg. Performed first on May 13, 2008.

FINALE

"Don't Let the Sun Go Down on Me" by Elton John, "In this Moment" (original composition sent in for the songwriting competition), and "Imagine." Performed last on May 20, 2008.

David Cook and I together at the end of the American Idol journey

People ask me all the time if I was upset because I didn't win the title of American Idol. I don't know why it's so hard for everyone to understand that making it to the finals with such an amazing singer felt humbling, and I was just honored that anyone would consider me to be at his level. As I said before, I always tried to take away the sense of competition from my motivation, and instead focused on the fact that I was in a great learning experience in the company of great talent. To me, that was already as gratifying as the idea of being chosen to be the American Idol. The fact that I had come this far was a personal accomplishment that went way beyond what I originally thought I was capable of, so the winning part of it just didn't matter at all.

I even remember telling myself, "David, don't be upset when you don't win 'cause it's going to be fine." Not "Don't be upset if you don't win"—it was clearly "when you don't win." How could I know? The truth is that just as I got an overwhelming feeling to go on that first audition in San Diego, I also knew at the finale in Los Angeles that I was not going to win. Don't ask me how, but I simply knew that it wasn't going to happen. It was a gut feeling, and by now you probably know where I stand on gut feelings. It's not that I think I made mistakes, I simply think I wasn't supposed to win. I wouldn't have done anything differently, because I sincerely believe that it was not my destiny to win that night. That was the beauty of it: I didn't expect to win. So when I didn't, I was totally prepared. I know this may be hard for many people to believe, but I don't think I even wanted to win. Winning would be too much of a responsibility, and honestly, I didn't know if I'd be ready.

I actually think I would've felt horrible if I had won, because I deeply felt that David Cook was the one who deserved it. Here was this amazing singer and all-around musician, someone I really looked up to and admired not just for his music side, but also as a person. I really respected him and the way he acted throughout the whole time we were together; I have to be honest and say that he was the person who, in my view, showed better than anyone else in the season that he should win. I was genuinely happy for him. And to top it all off, the first thing he said to me after he won was, "Love ya, bud. Thanks for being so awesome." I could not believe it. That's exactly what a winner should be, I thought. He showed such maturity in the way he treated me and everyone else on the show. He still treats me with so much respect, and to this day, I am proud of and happy for him for achieving all the success he has experienced.

I'm sure people thought that winning would have meant everything in the world to me, but I look at things a bit differently. I like to believe that you don't need to reach a certain goal to be happy. I prefer to think that happiness is always there, and that when things don't go the way we might like them to, it's a sign from above that something even better is right around the corner. Not winning was almost like a personal lesson on how to stay positive and optimistic. I think that's hard for people to understand. They wonder, "After all the hard work you put in, how can you be happy to be in second place? Why aren't you devastated?" And my answer to that is, "Well, why shouldn't I be happy? Over one hundred thousand people auditioned, and I never thought I would even get past the first round. Now here I am, months later, in front of millions of people, in the Top 2. How could that possibly be a bad thing? I may not have won, but there are about one hundred thousand other people who didn't win either. And I was the runner-up and have a great feeling of satisfaction and accomplishment knowing I did my very best. How could that possibly be a loss? I made it so much farther than I thought I was going to, and I got to have a musical experience second to none, so at the end of the day, how could I not be completely happy?" But because we live in such a competitive world, I think people have a hard time understanding that. I keep trying to explain that the whole thing for me was essentially about being given the chance to share music with others, because that's one of the things in life that makes me happiest. That's why I tried out to begin with. Everything else was icing on the cake.

In fact, I won something very precious on *American Idol*: the belief that when I sing, people actually enjoy it. As a kid, I never in my wildest dreams imagined that anyone could possibly be into my singing, so when it hit me that many people actually like my sound, it gave me a new sense of affirmation that I would carry moving forward. It was amazing to see that I could share something that means so much to me with other people, and that it makes them feel good, too. I learned that if you do the very best you can, you will eventually get to where you need to go. Sometimes that means you have to step out of your comfort zone; sometimes that means you have to take a chance; and sometimes that means you have to make mistakes. But the mistakes teach you.

Even though I had lost, I had won after all.

The night David Cook won the seventh season of *American Idol* turned out to be filled with all kinds of surprises. At the end of the show, after nineteen really challenging songs and so many days of some serious working and praying, I was relieved that it was finally over and I could go back to some degree of normalcy. Or not . . .

I went backstage after the show and sat in my dressing room trying to begin simmering down from the rush of the last six months. My studio teacher had a slice of pizza waiting for me because I had basically given up all dairy products for the duration of the show. Dairy always had a weird effect on my singing, so I played it safe and stayed away that whole time. The smell of that perfectly greasy pizza brought with it the reality that I could finally rest. Sure, I knew I was slated to go on the *American Idol* tour, but not having to compete made that seem like a walk in the park after what we had all been through. I felt more accomplished than I ever had in my life, more sure that I was definitely on the right path. Life as an *Idol* contestant was over and life as David Archuleta could now finally resume. My dad came in with a worried look on his face, then relief as I gave him a look that reassured him I was totally fine, relaxed and content.

But just as I was thinking about having a chance to relax and chill out a bit, Simon Fuller, the show's creator, came busting into my dressing room followed by a group of record label executives, everyone worked up, talking fast and loud. "As far as we're concerned there is more than one winner here tonight," Mr. Fuller said excitedly. There was a frenzy of hugs, handshakes and congratulations, all of which baffled me, until it hit me that the commotion was not just to make me feel good about coming in second. In fact, I was in the process of being signed by 19-E/Jive Records right there in the dressing room that very night! A record deal. Wow. This was the last thing that I expected to happen! In one second my little "hobby" turned into something real, something important, something valid. I was speechless, and I don't think I even had the stomach to finish the pizza with all the excitement buzzing in the room.

Even though I had lost, maybe I had won after all. I had shown everyone that my passion for music was real all the way to the end. The hard work had paid off, and the shadow of self-doubt was, at least for this moment, less than it had been in quite a while. My best, I'd learned, just might be good enough.

TOP 3 IDOL MEMORIES

▶ Singing "Imagine" for the first time was by far one of the most special moments, because back then I wasn't worried about anything. I was just happy to be there. It all felt so genuine.

▶ Day-to-day moments with the people who were in the show with me were some of the most special times I can remember—things like rehearsing songs together, or catching up on the rare occasions that we were on a break. These people were my friends and family for five months straight, and they made a tremendous impact on me. It was so inspiring to be among them all, and I'll always carry those memories close.

▶ The finale week was also a key moment for obvious reasons. The world was watching and there was no room for mistakes. There was so much energy in the air you could feel it; each performance required us to pour our souls into our songs. It was overwhelming in a way that I can't even begin to describe. We were now at the end of a journey and even though it was nerve-racking, it was incredibly exciting until the very end.

STEPPING IT UP

"You can't be confident when you are willing to stay within your own comfort zone. Confidence is built by pushing way beyond what you think you can do."

—BRYAN PULSIFER

7

Once the show ended there wouldn't be too much time to reflect, because just as quickly as the first phase of *Idol* was over, the next year of my life was instantly mapped out before my eyes. There would be no return to normalcy, only more craziness that would continue to totally blow me away. From the moment *Idol* ended it felt like someone had hit the fast forward button on my life, and it became clear that it wasn't going to slow down anytime soon. All I could do was brace myself and count my blessings.

Soon after the season wrapped, David Cook and I flew to New York to do a week of press. The whole media thing also took some getting used to. As I've never been much of a talker, speaking comfortably in front of cameras and doing interviews was a whole new world of nerves that I had to face. It seems to come naturally to so many performers, but unfortunately, I've never been one of them. I had to work very hard to feel ready for the constant and often repetitive questions from the press world, facing each interviewer confidently every time. *Idol* itself was a great training ground as we had several interviews each week and slowly but surely it did get easier. We went to the *Today* show where we were both able to perform out on the Plaza. We also visited with MTV, did several press events, and had some great food! I really enjoy New York and being able to walk out of your hotel to find a great restaurant on almost every block: Thai food, Italian food, amazing delis, and always some new and interesting restaurant to discover. Plus I just love the energy and fast pace of New York.

After the media blitz in New York, I only had one week off before having to go back to Hollywood to prepare for the *Idol* Summer Tour. I went to Lake Powell with my friends for a few days, which at first I didn't even want to do. I really thought I wanted to just be with my family for the week, but I realized it would be great for me to have an actual vacation where I got away completely and had time to just relax and enjoy one of the most beautiful places on earth. There were so many things brewing that I was afraid I couldn't afford to rest; I was on a serious roll. But my parents insisted. "You need to go. You need a break." The fact is, they couldn't have been more right. I *did* need a break, even just a short one, to think about what was going on and try to take it all in. Intellectually I knew that a relaxing week would be the best thing that could happen to me after the madness of the previous six months—and in the end I have to admit it was nice to get away from all the craziness—but it was also stressful because I felt the pressure of having an album to record. Even though I was technically on vacation, I not only had to work on some stuff for the tour, but also for my own album.

TOP 3 INTERVIEWS

► One of the funniest interview moments for me was during *American Idol* when someone asked me a question and I answered it, but for some reason everyone thought that I was going to keep on talking—only I was done talking. There was this awkward pause, and I looked at the interviewer, and everyone looked at me, and no one seemed to know what was happening for a moment.

► During the Jingle Bash radio show on B96 in Chicago, there was this funny DJ who kept asking me about my dating life and my love interests. She was so eager to get me talking, so I totally turned it around on her and started asking her about *her* dating life. It was hilarious.

► Another amazing interview was on Z100 in New York when they debuted my first-ever single, "Crush." It was finally my chance to present my first song to the world, and I was so nervous and excited. It was such an amazing feeling to be able to do that. I was all tingles for that entire interview.

And I wasn't only going to record songs, but I was also going to be able to write them myself. During my vocal paralysis period, my dad strongly encouraged me to work on my songwriting and piano abilities, which was what the record execs had advised me to do. I did write three songs during that period, but I always felt I wasn't very good at songwriting because it took me a long time to write each song, sometimes almost a year before I felt it was complete. It would turn out to be a good exercise though, because now I would have the opportunity to write with some world-class writers and at least I had already been through the process before. I knew it was finally time to start working on the next phase of my musical evolution, and writing for my own album was that logical next step. The label was pushing it, and honestly, despite my fears, I was also feeling ready to give it a go. The truth is that I always wanted to write my own music; I just never thought I was good enough, but now I had an opportunity to try it again. I felt the next chapter coming toward me like a massive snowball that seemed to be traveling at a wild speed, gaining momentum and size with every moment that passed. I wasn't prepared for any of it, and I definitely didn't have a vision. Things were being thrown so fast in my direction that I simply had to find a way to deal with everything on the spot. It was kind of like learning in real time.

. . . it felt like someone had hit the fast forward button on my life . . .

After years of telling myself that I wasn't ready, I was forced to be ready. I was forced to step up and accept the full responsibility that would come with this next phase of my musical "career." So while I was on vacation, I knew that no matter how much I wanted or expected things to wind down, there was no chance of that happening, at least

CHORDS OF STRENGTH

not anytime soon. There was a national three-month arena tour coming up that summer with the other top ten finalists. We were set to start rehearsing for that tour almost immediately after that brief week in Lake Powell. I had only a day or two at home, and then I was back with the other Top 10 Idols to get ready for the first show already slated for July 1. Then there was my solo album coming out in November, and a solo tour to promote it. These were things I associated with real stars. Not only was it impossible to imagine myself in that context, but I also realized it was going to be a huge challenge as to how to combine being a regular teenager with this new schedule and crazy agenda. There was absolutely nothing regular about anything that was happening.

I didn't quite understand how I could actually have arrived at this point until I started to see that every moment of my life had built on the previous one, creating this really cool chain link of experiences. I began to see the pattern of events as connected to everything that was happening in the present, which made me look to the future with even more excitement. It was scary; but at the same time I knew that I had finally gotten to a place that validated all my stops along the way. I was able to look back and see how every performance of my life—big or small—was a piece of the puzzle whose picture would be revealed one day in the form of my future. Despite all of my doubts and fears, I could now embrace that it was all well worth it, that God did have a plan for me, and that I did the right thing by trusting in Him. I would try to make sense of everything by always reminding myself that all of this was happening because I was following those impressions that I received from the Spirit along the way.

Once we got back to California to rehearse, I was very happy to know that we were going to be able to pick our own songs to perform on tour. We were also finally able to sing the full versions of the songs, and we were pretty much going to each do our own mini-concert. I was able to choose four songs for my set, so I thought it would be good to have a variety of songs both from the show as well as one that I hadn't performed before but had always wanted to. I brainstormed with my dad and we worked out some ideas for the arrangements and I decided to go ahead and play the piano on one of the songs. I decided to start off my set with "Angels," complete with fog machines as the piano and I would rise from the ground as the music began. I then performed "Apologize," which was one of my favorite moments on the show when I sang it with Ryan Tedder and One Republic, then "Stand by Me," which is just one of the greatest happiest songs ever. My set ended with "When You Say You Love Me," which is a song I was going to sing back in my *Star Search* days but never actually performed anywhere. It is also a song that has just so much feeling and emotion and very meaningful lyrics, so I thought it would be a great way to end my set, and let my fans and all my supporters know how they make me feel.

We rehearsed for the summer tour in Burbank at a large sound studio. The people running the show brought in the actual set so we could practice the way the show was actually going to happen. We only had four rehearsals each, but it turned out to be enough and the whole thing worked out perfectly. I felt ready, although a little nervous, but I couldn't wait to get out on the road. This tour would take us not only to U.S. cities but we were also going to make a stop in Canada, which was super-exciting because I had never been there before. The chance to travel and see new places was a perfect (and totally unexpected) cherry on top of everything else that was happening. I thought it was pretty cool to have been to New York, Los Angeles and Chicago as a kid, but now I was getting the chance to see the whole country—while I was singing the whole time! There would be two shows in Utah, so I would get to sing for my beloved home state that had been so supportive of me.

For the three months on tour, we lived like nomads, but we did stay in some really nice hotels. Even though I was only seventeen, I think I adjusted pretty well. I had moved around a lot when I was a kid, so I

This is me on tour feeling a whole lot better about myself as a singer

was used to changing environments. We lived in eight different houses when I was growing up, and now I was going to be able to live on a bus with my *Idol* family, the new tour crew and of course, my dad.

There were so many incredible things about the tour, starting with the fact that we were no longer in competition with one another. We could just let loose, have fun, and for the first time in months, sing

TOP 3 TOURING MOMENTS

▶ Performing in my hometown of Utah for the first time was amazing. In fact, I read that Utah crowds were known for being extra-spirited. That makes me proud. I remember being so emotional when we arrived in Utah on the *American Idol* tour. I sang "When You Say You Love Me," and it was so nice to get that special feeling of appreciation right at home.

▶ Something else that always strikes me when I'm on tour is meeting some of the people who come out to see me. I'm amazed when I meet these little kids who are so sweet and honest and will tell you their whole life story if you let them. Especially people who are going through a hard time. It always feels great to know that you're making other people feel better. I have to say that my best moments are not always onstage, but often offstage after the shows when we get to meet some of the fans.

▶ I also really loved my show in the Philippines, not just because it was such a massive show with more than eighty thousand people, but because of the people! It was nothing like anything I could have ever expected. First of all, I never imagined the Filipino people were going to be so fanatical, genuinely supportive and react to me the way they did—I didn't think they would even know who I was, but instead they treated us like royalty. How could they support me from so many miles away? It was mind-blowing and an unforgettable experience!

totally without fear. We had already spent so much time bonding during the show that this felt like a perfect vacation with the closest of friends, a chance to enjoy the closeness and collaboration we had created while on the show. I spent a lot of my time with Jason Castro and Kristy Lee Cook, but I also liked to go off on my own sightseeing adventures on those rare occasions when I'd have a few moments to myself.

Since we were usually on the bus, it was nice to have a morning when I could get out and walk around a bit, maybe get something to eat, and just take in the new environment like a tourist. It was refreshing to have this time, even though once in a while people would stop me on the street for an autograph, or to take a picture with them. I didn't mind; by now I knew it was all part of the deal.

I'll always remember being in Portland, Oregon, for the first time and walking around with Jason, taking in the vibe of the city, which

There were so many incredible things about the tour

I loved from the moment we arrived. We visited bookstores and just wandered around, loving the chance to be in this really cool new place. I also remember being in Pittsburgh and going running one morning and kayaking that same afternoon, which was so much fun and totally spontaneous. I had never been to Northern California either, which was so cool to finally see.

On many of the stops, though, we didn't get to even see the city we were in; the only place we'd visit was the arena where we'd be performing, because we needed time to sound check, rehearse and make sure that everything was running smoothly. The tour was like being in a routine that was different from *American Idol*. On the show so much was always being thrown at you at once, but on the tour things felt slightly less hectic.

Our main agenda was to perform, sign autographs and maybe do some press along the way. In a way, it was actually really relaxing. For me, the tour also represented everything about *Idol* that I loved so much: It brought together diverse talents to show the beauty of music, and without the element of a contest, so the experience (for us as well as the fans) was totally pure. On tour, I had the chance to learn some critical concepts, such as the importance of pacing myself, of interacting with fans, and I even had to learn the art of signing autographs. I actually changed my signature a few times until I found one that I could do fairly quickly, but still have it look like my name. The tour gave me a first taste of what life would be like as a professional singer. It taught me about the strength of discipline required to get from one day to the next and about the critical need to stay on course. Even better, being onstage so often continued to chip away at my confidence issues, giving me a chance to get comfortable with all the new attention. I was freer, more joyful, less nervous and generally more at ease with the idea of being in the spotlight. I was really starting to enjoy it. I was finally starting to let go and enjoy the act of performance just as much as I enjoyed singing. The *Idol* tour was an absolute gift that ultimately prepared me for my upcoming solo tour by giving me a chance to loosen up as an entertainer. Being surrounded by my *Idol* family made the whole thing feel entirely safe and comfortable, which I think made me stronger as an artist and helped to get me ready for everything that would come next.

I was freer, more joyful, less nervous

There didn't seem to be enough days in the calendar for all of the tasks ahead of me. I had signed with 19-E/Jive in June and they wanted an album out fast. I couldn't imagine how we could start production on an album that didn't even have a concept yet!

While I had lots of experience as a singer by now, I was still clueless as to what it would take to produce a record. I had always imagined that an album was the kind of thing you really take your time with, something you sit with and think about, with the sole purpose of letting yourself get inspired gradually and organically. I pictured a total creative immersion that would leave little time for anything else. I imagined I would get the chance to really explore the kind of music I wanted to put out, with enough time to create something truly unique that would reflect my taste and musical point of view.

Surprise—my first album would come about under entirely different circumstances. They wanted it out by November, so production needed to start right away. This meant writing, rehearsing and recording a good part of the album *while* I was on the *American Idol* tour. Deliberation was out and fast decisions were in. I didn't know the first thing about making a record, so the notion of making it happen while performing on tour seemed completely crazy (and borderline impossible) to me. Where would the inspiration come from? How would I know what kinds of songs to write? How could I know that those songs would be right for me? When would the rehearsing happen? Would I not be totally beat from the tour? How could I produce quality music in such a state of exhaustion? Every morning on the tour would bring on a bunch of new questions that would simmer in the back of my mind while I sat on the tour bus heading to our next gig. How would I know if I was doing everything right? How was I supposed to find and hire a team of professional music people? We didn't really have one yet. That's where my dad proved to be a big help while we were on tour. He was able to help with the recording process, kicking ideas around for songs and also helped with the difficult task of putting together our professional support team. We also had to schedule in meetings— while we were on tour—with potential attorneys, publishers, management companies, business managers, and all the other components that an artist needs in order to roll out a successful career.

To meet the deadlines for the album, I recorded wherever we happened to be—in Tulsa, Oklahoma City, Minnesota, and New York.

I would record during the day and perform with the rest of the *Idol* gang at night. I remember thinking, *Be careful what you wish you for,* because here I was living the life of a professional musician, including the sleepless nights, early mornings, press appearances and a constant pursuit of inspiration and endurance that I could only hope and pray would continue to come. It's funny how when you stop to look back, you tend to remember the moments of struggle. As I worked on both the tour and the album, I was forced to confront the nature of sacrifice, and face the fact that in choosing the path before me, my life, as I knew it, would no longer exist. I would have to give up being a regular eighteen-year-old and throw myself into adulthood, into the worlds of contracts, conference rooms, lawyers and so many other things that I don't really understand. I would have to get used to losing my privacy and feeling observed even when I didn't want to be observed. I would have to learn how to smile even when I was sad. I would have to put the brakes on any plans for college; and I would have to commit to staying focused and serious about my new career as a singer/songwriter with little distraction. I would have to be away from my friends and family a lot of the time, and I would have to find a way to keep those important relationships alive. I would basically have to put my normal life on the back burner, which felt (and sometimes still does) like a pretty big deal to me.

There was just no time to sit back and *think*. It was a challenge, but I was so grateful for the fact that from the moment I woke up to the instant I went to sleep my day revolved around music. All the questions that I had about my future were now less scary to look at, because somehow or another I started to feel that no matter what, music would always be a part of my life. I told myself that the pressure to deliver on the album while on tour was maybe the kind of heat that I needed to make it all happen. I chose to see the challenge as motivation, which would come in handy because, as I already mentioned, the next rung on the ladder of progress for me would come in the form of . . . gulp . . . songwriting.

Courtesy of Amy Wilson

Since I was ten years old, people had been advising me to write songs and it was one of those things I knew I should take seriously. But it always scared the life out of me. It was hard for me at age thirteen or fourteen, and it's still hard for me now (but getting easier). As connected as I am to music, for some reason I find it grueling to sit down and write melodies and lyrics. Melodies are a bit easier, but lyrics have always been an obstacle for me. Maybe it's because I am still young and have a lot to learn about music and life, but I have always found it easier to slip into the sentiment of a song as opposed to trying to come up with it myself. I feel comfortable putting myself in other people's shoes, and uncomfortable when I have to express myself in my own words.

Courtesy of Jennifer Uriegas

I told myself that since feeling itself has always been my guiding force, I could start with that as a basis for writing, too. Instead of trying to come up with clever words to tell a story, maybe I could focus more on an emotion, and somehow find the words that match the feeling. Maybe I could even use my own frustration as a songwriter and put *that* feeling into the song. Who knew? Maybe I could use my excitement to fuel the creative flow. There are so many ways to go about it and the more I thought about it, the more I realized that there isn't just one right way to do it.

Besides, the record company had its own ideas about what my first solo album should be, so whether I liked it or not I had a set of guidelines to work with. I didn't care so much about what labels I would be filed under; I just wanted to keep on singing. Ultimately, the album became a nice compromise between Jive's ideas and mine; while they were more inclined to a smooth pop sound, I leaned toward something a little bit deeper. But I was there to learn as much as possible, and back then I wasn't about to argue about any of it. I mostly saw the album as a chance to prove to myself that I was someone who could sing way beyond standards and covers. And I wanted to show the world that I was still a teenager and that I had no interest in growing up too fast. The songs on the first album would end up being about simple, universal things like first loves and crushes, themes that everyone can relate to.

The energy of the tour and all the amazing people around me also fed into the writing and recording that I was doing. Because there was so much musical energy around me, I felt connected to music in a very immediate way. I was living and breathing it, and the company of such talented singers inspired me every day as I continued to work through the album. My first single, "Crush," came out in August on Z100, New York City's famous radio station, while I was still on tour with *American Idol*. It was crazy to think that I had a song, *my own song,* on the airwaves. Would people even recognize that it was me? How would they react? How could they possibly like a song that was recorded so fast, and by such a rookie? I was

Courtesy of Emily Harmon

Courtesy of Emily Harmon

scared that I wouldn't be taken seriously outside the world of *Idol*. I even wondered if my fans would like it because it was a completely new style for me. It felt like such a huge risk.

Despite all my doubts, "Crush" somehow ended up at number two on the Billboard Hot 100. I was totally psyched. To my complete shock, they also said it was the best chart debut in more than eighteen months, and I had a really hard time understanding them fully. We were not even finished with the whole album, and the single was already out and to my surprise, it seemed to be doing well! It soon became apparent that this would be the rhythm of my life for a while—fast and furious—and if I wanted to play the game, I would have to accept this madness as part of the rules.

If touring and recording weren't enough for a newbie like myself, there was also the video for the single to shoot—a whole new challenge for a guy who can barely get a sentence out to a reporter, let alone *act*. I was afraid of becoming the laughingstock of YouTube, and I felt paranoid about the idea of having so many people watch me squirm out of my comfort zone. It was a terrifying but crucial part of the process, especially if we wanted the single to continue to do well. But I was always so uncomfortable in front of the cameras; I just didn't know how I was going to tackle this new beast.

We shot the video in Atlanta on one of my days off from the tour. I had a show the day before and another one the day after, so the pressure was on; we had to make sure we got all the shots right. It was a beautiful summer morning, and the plan was to shoot just as the sun was coming up, which of course made for excellent inspiration. I thought: *All I have to do is sing like I know how to sing, and try to let loose.*

In the end, it was a lot less stressful than I thought it would be, and way more fun than I ever could have expected. I have family on my mom's side that lives in Atlanta, so my dad surprised me by having the whole family fly out to see my first video shoot as well as go to a few shows in Atlanta and Tampa. It was so nice to be all together, if only for a few days, and it felt incredibly supportive to have my relatives there while I was working on this latest challenge. It taught me that sometimes the anticipation of something is a lot worse than the actual thing itself.

I was afraid of becoming the laughingstock of YouTube

In hindsight, I can see how important the video was in giving my song another dimension, another element for the audience and fans to hold on to, and a chance to watch me perform. I've already talked about why I think you should not only listen to a singer but watch as well. The making of the video got me thinking about the interpretation of the song in a more exacting manner, paying more attention to my facial expressions and body language, and bringing in a bit more drama and character to punctuate some of the song's key moments. It was actually kind of cool.

What was missing was the one variable that has always fueled my shows: a live audience. Without someone to sing for, I wasn't sure how I would work up the right energy. After all, it was always the looks in the eyes of the people out in the audience that gave me direction when I sang. It was their appreciation that kept the fire burning for me during each show. How could I do it without them? I literally had to pretend that I was singing for a room full of people to get the song right and in the end it all worked out wonderfully. Though at first I had stressed out about the video, after all was said and done, I not only learned a lot but also had a total blast making it happen.

One thing I find to be kind of tricky is understanding the world of fans. It's hard to understand how people who have never even met me can realistically like me so much. I mean, how can you get so excited about a person you know virtually nothing about? It was especially odd to hear that someone could actually have a crush on me without knowing who I really was! The whole idea nagged at me a bit. It made me question the nature of stardom, and start thinking about how I wanted people to see me as an artist. I didn't want to be seen only as

Courtesy of Elsa Tovar

Here I am posing with a group of super friendly fans

TOP 3 FAN ENCOUNTERS

▶ I'll always remember the little girl I met through the Make-a-Wish Foundation. She had cancer and said that one of her wishes was to hear me sing. She was also a singer and a cheerleader, just eleven years old, but she couldn't even open her eyes; she was so weak. I remember she was trying so hard just to smile. It just put everything into perspective for me. I didn't want to disappoint her. She was beyond a fan. She was a sweet soul who wanted to be comforted by music she loved. She was going through chemotherapy, and she knew music would make her feel better. I have so much respect for that, and was honored to be able to share that moment with her. Three days later she passed away, and I always look back at that moment with strong emotion.

▶ Some of my best fan encounters are when people actually say something like "Thank you for singing that song; I really felt something when you sang it." That always makes me feel reassured somehow, and reminds me of why I'm doing this to begin with.

▶ One time while I was on the *American Idol* tour in Pennsylvania, this girl came up to me after a show and gave me a diverse array of obscure kitchen utensils: an avocado slicer, a cherry pitter, and some other thing for corn, too. I thought, "Well, that's certainly special." It reminded me of how interesting and dynamic people can be.

a teen heartthrob who catered to crying girls; I wanted to sing for as many people as would listen. But the "fan-omenon," just like everything else, had its pros and cons, and I ultimately made up my mind to stay optimistic about the mania, accepting the positive things about it and simply observing and acknowledging any negativity or weirdness that it might also bring about. Besides, it was something that was completely out of my control, so there was no use trying to fight it!

At every concert, there were many young girls out in the audience, true, but there were also grandparents out on a date; I'd see groups of friends, colleagues and entire families. There were girls, boys, men and women of all ages, which gave me the sense that there really was a universal tone and message to my singing. I was able to finally see that the best thing *American Idol* had given me (besides some confidence and a more sharpened sense of self) was a wide audience. Through being on the show, I learned the invaluable lesson that music has nothing to do with the way you look or what your age is. Music transcends those things. With a forum like *Idol* each and every one of us was able to show our best as singers, no matter who we were or where we came from. We were finally able to crawl out of the shadows of our own self-criticism and proudly step into the spotlight, where we could begin to share a little piece of our souls with anyone who was listening.

If I thought 2008 was crazy, the even crazier 2009 kicked off with my own solo tour, which was almost totally sold out. In twenty-seven appearances across the country, I had the chance to perform alone onstage, and I had a warm-up act, Leslie Roy, opening for me, which was really strange because I was a big fan of hers and loved her music. Many folks in the audience knew the songs, and even the lyrics, from my album. But there were also a lot of people who didn't know the music and were hearing it live for the first time, which I took as a total compliment. The idea that someone would come to my show without even knowing the music! Now that's dedication, I thought.

It was really weird for me to accept the reality that I had actual fans. Not just *Idol* fans, but fans that would come out just to see me. It seemed completely crazy to me that so many people would even know who I was, let alone make such an effort to express their appreciation. Where were all of these kind words coming from? How could a shy eighteen-year-old matter to them? I had begun as part of the *American Idol* show, but now, for the first time, I was being given the chance to be *me*. I realized that, along with having a relationship with music, I'd now be able to have a very solid relationship with my fans. Each time I faced an audience, no matter where I was, would prove this to be true. There were some people I began to see over and over again. Why would they want to see me more than once? Why would they travel all over to show their support? Once again, I was blown away. I have always

Courtesy of Lois Alksninis

The fans are always the ones who keep me going

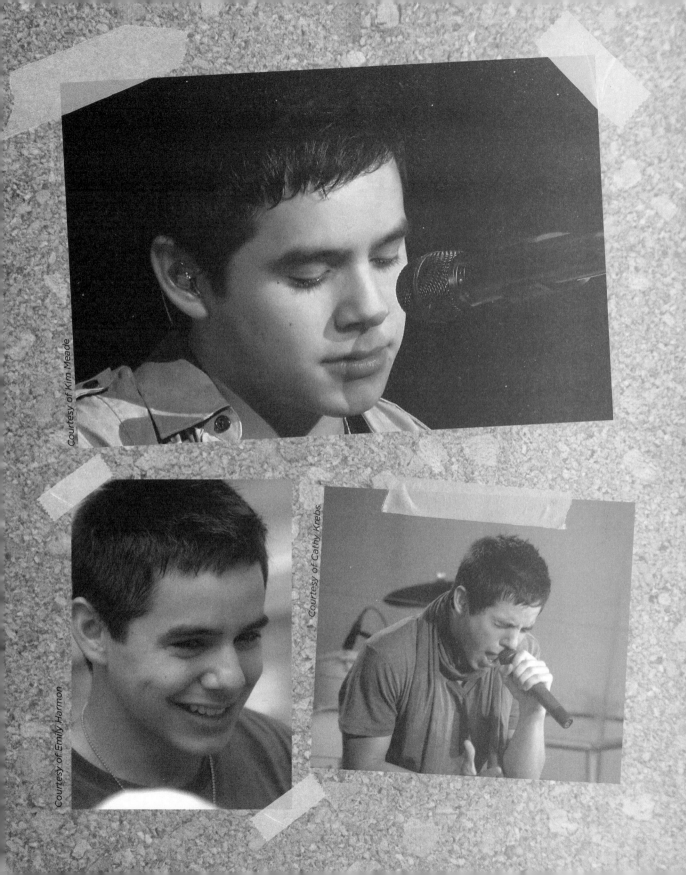

Courtesy of Kim Meade

Courtesy of Emily Harmon

Courtesy of Cathy Krebs

felt that without the fans, I had no way of completing the experience of singing, that without them, I would still be the shy kid in the back-yard who felt safe singing to his cats. My fans allowed my music to become part of an exchange, which made me feel that someone would always be listening. I owe this ongoing experience to the world's great-est group of fans!

There have been so many fans and from all over the world. People have come from Singapore, the UK, Canada, China, Japan, Germany, Italy, the Philippines, Denmark, Israel, Malaysia, Puerto Rico, Mexico, and so many others that as much as I want to, I can't even keep track! It seemed that many of the fans wanted to go out of their way to make sure I knew just how strongly they felt about me. It was almost as if they picked up on my insecurities and worked extra-hard to make sure that I'd feel good about myself. More than fans, they felt like a team of morale-boosters who would always be around to remind me of my worth. The fans stepped up as the much-needed providers of faith and motivation that I would come to rely on as I continued down this new path.

DIVINE FREQUENCY

"We are not human beings on a spiritual journey. We are spiritual beings on a human journey."

—STEPHEN R. COVEY

Sometimes, in this constantly evolving world of pop music, I find it important to continually remind myself of my original motivation for singing. For me, singing has also been a tool for something else, something more profound, even spiritual.

No matter what song I perform, my primary goal is to communicate with the audience, transfer feelings to them, and then have the energy they feel come back to me again. This, to me, is the coolest thing about performing. First the energy starts up; then it just builds and builds until the band and I feel excited, and then to see the audience also experience something incredible makes my role as a performer seem almost perfect. A lot of what I try to accomplish musically has to do with the type of song I choose to sing. Some are happy, some are sad. Some songs are just quirky and fun. "Touch My Hand," "Works for Me" and "Zero Gravity" are songs I love to perform. They aren't meant to be too serious, they're just meant for everyone to jump around or clap or just have a good time. Other types of songs that I enjoy singing are more about relationships like "Crush," and "Barriers," or romantic ballads like "To Be with You" and "You Can." There are other songs that have special messages and can really touch and move people in a very emotional and even spiritual way like "Angels," "Imagine," "Fields of Gold," certain Christmas songs and "Prayer of the Children." As much as I love all kinds of music, I've always had a special place in my heart for this last type of songs.

So as I think back on it now, I think it is safe to say that music is something you both hear and feel. I also realize that feelings change frequently and that for the most part, they are not a constant. They change from high to low, happy to sad, content to ecstatic and back down again. Not all music has the same purpose, but most music makes you feel "something." I personally love the type of music that has the ability to lift and heal and inspire. I've always responded emotionally to music, but there are certain songs that go beyond just fun or pretty or sad. There are songs that make me feel something so strong that while I am performing, it's almost like I am being transported to somewhere else and for a few minutes I feel like I am inside that song, trying to pour out as much emotion and energy as I can. Not everyone feels it the same way, but some people seem to connect at a very deep level. They too become a part of the moment, and the song seems to embrace them as well, and does something that borders on a spiritual experience. When the intent and emotions of the song are right, I get swallowed up in that emotion, and it helps me know for sure that there is a power much higher than you or me that is in charge of all that is good in the world, including certain special types of music.

For me, it is a privilege to experience that mutual connection, not just between the audience and me, but sometimes also with God. It is the most satisfying part of being able to perform music. This is a very sacred subject for me, so I hope I can express adequately what I really feel because I believe that I have a responsibility to use the passion that I have for music to do good. Let's start with the fact that I wouldn't even be in the position to write this book had it not been for *American Idol*, which, as you know, I would never have done had I not first pondered and prayed about it. I like to think of prayer as a way of getting advice from someone who knows my true purpose and wants to help me grasp and more fully understand what that purpose is. Faith has played a really important role in my journey, at each moment arming me with strength to push forward to the next level. At each step along the way I would make it a point to thank God for all that He's done, and to pray for the strength I'd need to make it through to the next phase. I knew that my commitment to trusting in Him would become the compass that would keep my course steady, and that with this belief close to my heart, I would be able to keep my motives and actions in check. I try to think about how a song will impact other people positively or negatively and make sure that my values come across to whoever listens to it. It's like when I just try to do what's right, the Lord blesses me both directly and also indirectly by also blessing other people. You can see how it helps other people and that is the most satisfying part of it. I think since I was a little boy, I have understood these concepts subconsciously. And when I had the

> # I find it important to continually remind myself of my original motivation for singing.

challenges of vocal paralysis, even though I knew I would probably be happy learning a variety of other professions, I still felt that nothing was ever quite as special as music. But even with the challenges I faced during that time, some good has come even from the problems I had with my strange, messed-up vocal cord. My current vocal coach thinks that there are still some residual effects from the partial paralysis. The doctor showed us that one cord is at more than full strength and the other one still has some problems; but he also says it gives my voice a distinct sound. "Some singers have a quirk that gives their voice a unique quality," he told me. "And this has done that for you." Even that seemingly horrendous diagnosis has turned into a kind of blessing. When I really look at it, I tend to wonder if God's hand was involved in this. Probably, but I don't want it to sound like God made

Courtesy of Kim Meade

Always trying to stay connected to the divine frequency

CHORDS OF STRENGTH

me have vocal paralysis in order to then miraculously fix me. It's more like He gave me the ability to persist, despite the challenges that were also part of my path.

But the vocal condition was only one snag in my path. Sure, I always loved to sing, but in my mind that didn't necessarily add up to a promising future in the music industry. It was totally the opposite: I never thought I had the skills to deliver in true "star" fashion. You already know that I had serious confidence issues, and I always found it difficult to express myself. It was a challenge for me to articulate my ideas about music, or anything for that matter—I saw myself as too shy, too quiet, too introspective, too much of the stuff that pop stars are *not* made of. So it was definitely a strange little conflict that I lived with: On the one hand, I sang obsessively; but on the other hand, I cringed at the sound of my own voice and belittled my potential as a serious singer. I saw myself as a die-hard *fan* of music and singing, more than actually being someone who could be a professional singer. I did want it but, sadly, I never imagined that I could have it. There were always going to be singers out there who were more skillful, more talented and more suited for a life onstage, I thought, and I would never be able to measure up to their level. I would never have the confidence or stage presence skills that seemed to come so naturally to the singers I admired.

> **I try to think about how a song will impact other people positively or negatively and make sure that my values come across to whoever listens to it.**

But I did have desire and faith that if I shared my talent, good would come from it, for others as well as myself—which I believe are the two main reasons why I was able to overcome anything at all. Through that desire and faith I managed to bridge this gap between my personality and my passion.

You see, the fact that my love for singing came at such a very young age, and became such a passion for me starting with my fascination with *Les Misérables*, the desire and joy I felt singing was something that I could never deny. If God gave me the desire to sing, I figured there must be a pretty good reason for it. I chose to have faith in Him and His reasons (whatever they may be), and let this faith fuel my decisions and behavior. By sticking to this idea I would always have a spiritual compass. By leaning on God, fear would be replaced with courage; doubt with hope; and uncertainty with the acceptance of the fact that we don't always know where we are going or why we're heading in a particular direction. But if we trust in Him, He will lead us to the place where we are supposed to go. I was able to internalize the reality that sometimes we can be our own worst enemies, but with His help we can get ourselves out of our own way. I definitely can say that without this spiritual perspective, I just wouldn't be where I am now.

When I think back on it: At first I needed the help of God to decide if I should take the first step to cross a critical bridge. Then I needed His assistance to actually cross the bridge. And finally, when I got to the other side of that bridge, it turned out I needed Him the most. Now in this strange new spotlight, I cling to my spiritual connection more than ever. The world I was thrown into thanks to *American Idol* was one that could easily reprogram a person's sense of normalcy, potentially chipping away at one's most important values. Instead, I like to direct my energy into remembering what life and happiness are really all about.

We all have our own way of seeing the world and dealing with the ups and downs that life gives us, and I think that part of being able to relate to as many people as possible is in accepting the differences and imperfections in us all. I believe that even though we all have issues and problems and bad habits and idiosyncrasies, we're here to learn

Courtesy of Kim Meade

Having a moment
with myself
before the show

and to better ourselves. We're all given different challenges, but we're all ultimately here to find true happiness; some people figure it out earlier in life than others, but it's never too late. We're here to work to find it and to help other people find it. We are supposed to care about one another and look at ways in which we can inspire and lift one another up when someone else needs it most. At the same time, we can't rely on others to do everything for us. We shouldn't just accept our station in life and think that we can't change where we are at. Even as we are working on ourselves, we should be encouraging one another to work things out and aspire for more. I want people to be hopeful and know that they have the potential to be happy in life. There may be many ways to achieve that, but we all need to work for it and strive to find it in our own way. It is hard to give someone happiness; it is something that you earn by your own actions, thoughts and beliefs, as well as through the way you treat yourself and others. I totally believe everyone in life is meant to be happy; and happiness really has to come from doing what is right and being there for others. No one can make you be happy all the time. You simply have to learn it for yourself.

I did have desire and faith . . .

Looking back on my vocal paralysis challenge, some people may think that it made me unhappy because I couldn't sing. The good thing is that despite my frustration, I was still happy because I had plenty of other things in my life that made me happy. So instead of being totally unhappy about the challenge I faced, I looked at it as an opportunity to learn more. I think that the fact of having some time off from singing actually prepared me for when *Idol* came around—it motivated me to work twice as hard. It gave me an opportunity to learn to be patient and think about a lot of other interesting things I could do with my life. I still loved and listened to music, and I wasn't going to stop and let it make me feel depressed. I just dealt with it and moved on and was planning to just be a normal kid and maybe study to become a veterinarian; later on I thought about being a dentist, and in high school I even thought about becoming an ear, nose, and throat doctor.

So when I finally "got my voice back," of course I was happy about it, but I also knew I couldn't take it for granted. I realized that I needed to show my appreciation and gratitude by using what I believed had been given back to me by God, and in a way that would help and benefit others and not just myself. When I prayed, I really believed I was able to speak with our Heavenly Father and that He would actually communicate back with me, which He did. I wanted Him to know how much I appreciated Him and His guidance and the talents and experiences He has allowed me to have. To this day, I want to involve him in all that I do, so I can keep things in the proper perspective without allowing pride or ego to creep in.

When I began on *Idol*, the reality of my crazy schedule and the new pace of things made it a very real challenge to stay grounded spiritually. For starters, the whole time we were in L.A., we were able to go to church only once or twice, a sacrifice that I made knowing that the Heavenly Father said that I should do this. I knew He understood, so although I felt badly about it, I knew He was aware that I would

> **I realized that I needed to show my appreciation and gratitude by using what I believed had been given back to me by God**

always think about him, listen for the promptings of His Spirit, and follow those whisperings. I promised myself that church or no church, I would keep God close, and though I wasn't in touch with too many people outside of the *Idol* world during those six months, my relationship with God was the one I worked on the most. I know that some people might have expected me to change somehow under these new, very Hollywood circumstances, but I knew that if I remained mindful of my spiritual needs and obligations, God would support me and provide me with the comfort, hope and feelings of joy that would sustain me. The guidance I received through the Spirit became the barometer against which I could measure everything that was happening, and it helped me keep all the tasks and responsibilities as a contestant on *Idol* in the proper perspective. I would be a contestant on *Idol* just for a short time, but I would be a son of my Heavenly Father forever. Because of this belief, I was better able to find meaning, purpose, comfort, peace and even happiness despite the chaos. He was and is my anchor, and I don't know how I would have survived any of all this without Him.

My goal was always to stay close to God

So even though there were times when I simply didn't think I'd be able to handle things, when the possibility of failure seemed more likely than my progress on the show, I knew I had to hang in there. Even though my goal was always to stay close to God, it wasn't always so simple to make it happen. Sometimes I was so overwhelmed with the process and schedule that I just didn't have enough time to recharge spiritually. It was so challenging to keep a balance when the schedule

CHORDS OF STRENGTH

Courtesy of Kim Meade

Feeling the fire here!

didn't allow it but I realized that I would have to fit in at least a little time for prayer and Scriptures. It was an important lesson to learn, because the moment I realized that I could always fit in some time with the Spirit, even if for just a few minutes, a huge burden of guilt and unworthiness was lifted off of me and I realized that from then I would make it a goal to always fit in some spiritual time every day, even if I didn't think there was time. I'm not going to say I have done this perfectly, but when I do it, it definitely pays off!

Having a spiritual foundation based on faith in a living God helps remind me that my life is not just about becoming a famous singer, but about what I can do to help other people feel good. I truly believe that God gave us music for a reason; I'm no expert, but I am pretty certain that reason has a lot to do with my happiness.

THE JOY IN SOUND

"The aim and final end of
all music should be none other
than the glory of God and the
refreshment of the soul."

—JOHANN SEBASTIAN BACH

"Music and rhythm find their
ways into the secret places of
the soul."

—PLATO

So many things confuse me. But "feeling" is a language I can understand. That's why I connect with music so much. Music contains such a broad range of emotions. Now that I think about it, I've always been really bad at writing papers. I would always finish last, and it would take me forever to organize my ideas and communicate them clearly. But feelings speak where words fail me, and that's what music does for me. It's a powerful way for me to communicate with people. I perceive the world through the wide range of emotions that whirl all around in it—and it's almost like my antennae for those emotions live inside my love for music. Music is a tool for expressing and communicating emotion. But it doesn't stop there: My hope is that when I perform live, my music is *received* by an audience, and that the audience is as affected as I am while I'm singing. To me this is the most beautiful thing about music—it is a give and take between performer and audience, an opportunity to share the emotions of that singular moment. It's always different, so each one of those moments is loaded with a sense of possibility and spontaneity, making the process totally organic and just so interesting, no matter how many times I do it.

My natural feelings *are* fluid, so it's important to keep the heart open and to be in the moment of any performance. Each show is a unique send-receive moment where all of the parties involved—singer and audience members—can jointly experience the sentiment of a song. The music itself *is* the connection. There are many millions of songs in the world, each one its own little bubble of feelings. Each time we sing, we are asked to communicate its emotional essence. You might say that music has the power to make us more compassionate, because it has this special ability to let us feel what the song's creator felt when he wrote it. It puts us all on the same emotional playing field.

The point I'm trying to make is that music can be so much more than just entertainment. It can be an act of communion, a dialogue in sound, sacred or soulful, happy or sad, intense or soothing; it can cover the entire spectrum of human emotions. With music we can all speak the same language and we can relate to one another's joys and pains. I recently learned the meaning of the word "catharsis," which the dictionary defines as "an experience of emotional release often inspired by or through art." It comes from the Greek word *"katharos,"* which literally means "pure." To me this is the perfect description of what happens through music on many occasions: There is an emotional release that comes along with (or maybe leads to) a total state of purity. As a singer I feel it quite often, and when I look out

> ... "feeling" is a language I can understand ...

CHORDS OF STRENGTH

Sometimes the silence between the notes hold just as much emotion as the melodies themselves

into the crowds, I can see when they feel it, too; it is a momentary and collective catharsis that packs a punch.

You might be thinking, "Okay, so music is feeling. Big deal." But the way I see it, because music is so deeply charged emotionally it has the power to be a very useful tool. Music can ignite deep happiness or profound sadness in one instant. It can change your mood by taking you to a special place inside. Music has the power to inspire nostalgia for things that we have lost and to remind us that they still live somewhere in our heart.

I remember that when I was eleven, the 2002 Winter Olympics came to our hometown of Salt Lake City. One night, we had the TV on, but we weren't really watching the figure skating program. It was the night Michelle Kwan did her last performance. The most beautiful song came on and we all stopped what we were doing so we could watch and listen to the way the beautiful skating matched the soothing and pure voice we all heard. The music was Eva Cassidy singing "Fields of Gold," which originally sounded much different when it was performed by Sting. When I heard Eva Cassidy sing, I felt like I was listening to the most beautiful music I had ever heard. It was just a guitar and her voice, no other instruments, and there was no need for anything else. It would have gotten in the way. I remember that my dad and I both were completely blown away at the level of sensitivity, dynamics, tone and just overall beauty that came through the TV when we heard that amazing music.

After that experience, of course we ran out and bought all the Eva Cassidy CDs we could find and listened to her music. At that point I realized she was someone special and that I wanted to learn to sing like she did. I wanted to be able to feel the range of emotion she demonstrated in each song she sang. We also found several familiar songs that she performed unlike the other versions we were familiar with. One of those was "Over the Rainbow," which we also heard on season two of *American Idol* when Kimberly Locke performed it. But the song that most touched me and made me want to sing like Eva was her rendition of John Lennon's "Imagine." It was so beautiful and simple. Her phrasing and nuances were perfect. The note choices and melodic changes were inspired and intuitive.

A couple of years later I decided to learn her version and perform it on a few occasions including a live performance on TV on ABC 4's *Good Things Utah*, after I was asked to perform on the show having been on *Star Search*. Of all the performers I have listened to, Eva Cassidy best represented the style and level of artistry that I would most aspire to. She had the whole package: She had tone, pitch, range, dynamics, and control, and she could sing any type of style from blues to folk to pop. You could totally feel her spirit when she sang and I hope someday to learn how to sing with as much expression and mastery as she did.

Here's another story: When I was younger, our family used to perform in hospitals and retirement homes. With our costumes and sheet music in hand, we would rip right through the dark frost of December with the warmth and cheerfulness of our little homegrown variety show. Some of our audience members were old, some were sick, and many were both— but all of their eyes would sparkle like shiny new Christmas ornaments each time one of us would get up to sing. My little sister, Jazzy, would put on a curly red wig and belt out "Tomorrow" from the popular show *Annie*. One of the numbers I'd sing was from the movie *Yentl*, a song called "A Piece of Sky," which had always been an Archuleta family staple given my grandma Claudia's admiration for Barbra Streisand. Though I didn't necessarily know what I was singing about, I knew exactly how that song made me feel—a raw sentiment that I saw reflected in the eyes of an elderly woman whose tears of appreciation slowly trickled down into her lap. She was in a wheelchair, she could barely talk, but here she was very touched by the song, perhaps transported to a happier time in her life when all was well. She later told us that the song instantly rekindled lost memories of her late husband, and gave her an unexpected feeling of happiness that day. Even though we were generations apart in age,

Courtesy of Kim Meade

Nothing feels better than knowing that by singing I can make others feel better

it was interesting to see how a song could bridge that gap and allow me to relate to her through the medium of a song. I could feel the melody soothe so many of this poor woman's pains, and I could see the lyrics fill her heart with peace. Here was that gift again, this time coming from me to her—and in that moment I realized that performing for me would be much more than just being a good singer, and everything to do with being a good person.

The bottom line is that while you're performing it's hard to hide who you really are. It's all about the interpretation of the song, not just the song itself. Some songs have been performed many times over by many different artists, but some were memorable and others were not. It's all about the connection between the performer, the song, the message and the audience. People are all so different; we come from all walks of life,

CHORDS OF STRENGTH

in all shapes, colors and sizes. The one thing we all have in common is our ability to feel and emote. When we hear a song, we feel the emotions of that song as it relates to our own personal experience, which I guess is why I see music as a great vehicle for compassion. If we can momentarily feel what others feel, we move farther and farther away from selfishness into a state of empathy and compassion. The bottom line is that music is healing, so I'm honored to be in any way part of that process.

Interpretation is the key component of being a successful singer. It requires that you capture the emotional language of a song, and then express it your own way for someone else. It is essentially being able to understand and relate to someone else's emotions, even if you yourself have never felt those emotions before. It's the reason why, when I was twelve years old on *Star Search* singing Alicia Keys' "Fallin'," I didn't have a clue in the world as to what I was singing about. (How could I? I was only a kid.) I was trying to get into the energy of that song, the soulfulness of the song, in a way that I hoped people could feel deeply. Because I've been singing from a very early age, I have frequently sung about things that I simply hadn't lived or been through yet. But it never seemed to matter because I could still internalize their feelings, relay them, which allowed other people to feel them too. I already told you that I think emotions are contagious, but when you throw music into the mix it becomes like a breeding ground for sensitivity.

I can't stress it enough that for me, being a recording artist has nothing to do with fame and everything to do with feelings. It always thrills me when I notice someone in the audience really feeling it. I can see that they are actually feeling what I'm singing about, which, to me, gives meaning to the whole act. It allows me to forget about the scary aspect of performing, and instead fuels me with motivation to keep going. It's so powerful that it can turn an intensely shy person (me) into someone who is willing to pour his heart out for arenas full of people. Music just tugs. It draws you in, allowing you to tap into the secret spaces of life that sometimes get lost in the day-to-day.

This really rang true for me when I turned on the television one day, only to discover the horror of September 11, 2001, being reported on every news station across the country. I was ten years old, so of course I couldn't (and still can't) totally comprehend the nightmare that was unfolding in New York and Washington, D.C. Even though it was all happening miles away from my peaceful world in Sandy, Utah, I felt the pain of those people deep in my gut, and I could feel a small piece of my innocence being ripped right out of me. My parents, like everyone else, were solemnly glued to the TV, desperate for more information. I would sit and watch with them, half traumatized, half clueless about what was happening. I was too young (and probably still am) to really understand the scope of that tragedy. I also remember all of us huddled together, watching the celebrity telethon that aired live after the attack. There was a sense of sorrow and anguish about every word spoken, a sadness that seemed to have the power to linger over us indefinitely.

Just as I was thinking about this dark reality, something amazing caught my attention: Celine Dion began to sing "God Bless America." Somehow, through the darkness, appeared a glimmer of light; the emotion in the music gave me a sense of hope. I was so impressed by how Celine was able to take a song that was so familiar and make it seem like it was the first time I had ever heard it. It was clear that that particular song had a very special meaning for us all. The events of those days made us all hear it, though with a new purpose and awareness.

It was another one of those moments when the power of song, combined with the truth about human emotion, came together in a way that felt totally healing. Once again I understood that a certain song could strike enough feeling to inspire the kind of therapeutic force that we need when bad things happen. The experience confirmed that for me, singing would be as much about conveying love as it would be about participating in art. Every time I would hold a microphone in my hand could be a unique opportunity to share from my heart, a chance to connect with an audience without even having to know anyone's name. For the rest of my life, I have known (consciously or

Courtesy of Kim Meade

Here I am looking serious as I belt it out

unconsciously) that performing, for me, will never be an act of personal self-indulgence but instead one of total connectivity.

A year later, as chance would have it, when I was in New York meeting with record labels, I had the privilege of being invited to sing at the Firefighters' Station 54 on the first anniversary of 9/11. I knew I was singing to people who had lost wives, husbands, fathers, mothers, daughters, sons, sisters and brothers, and when I sang for those people on that day, I felt their pain. Even though I couldn't possibly begin to understand what they'd gone through, I knew by the looks on the faces of the crowd that it was a moment loaded with raw emotion, a type of sadness unlike anything I'd ever seen. I wasn't sure what my place would be there, but the moment I started to sing, I understood. I sang "God Bless America" and "I Will Always Love You" and I left that group of people feeling deeply moved by the energy left in the air after I sang. It was one of those moments when music came in where words could not—when a melody could do for a person's soul what a string of spoken sentences would never be able to do.

Here was music stepping in, not as entertainment, but as genuine emotional help, an insight that would give meaning to the kind of singer I would always aspire to be.

I regularly find myself thinking about how crazy it is that all of this started for me when I was so young. I really wasn't able to understand a whole lot of what was going on at the time, but I recently was asked to respond to a clip of myself being interviewed when I was about eleven or twelve. Here's what I had to say: "I love singing because it makes people feel good and it makes me feel good inside. Everyone loves music."

Almost seven years have passed since I said those words, and it's safe to say that I believe I'm still the same person now that I was then. To this day, I feel exactly the same way about music as I did back then. I sing because it makes people feel good, and that is the truth.

STAYING TRUE

"Good character is more to be praised than outstanding talent. Most talents are, to some extent, a gift. Good character, by contrast, is not given to us. We have to build it, piece by piece."

—H. J. BROWN

10

Sometimes when I have a little bit of down-time (which isn't as often these days!), I like to think about what's really going on; what's really most important. I know it sounds pretty simple, but when I do this—when I actually stop and organize my thoughts and ponder the things that matter most—it helps me feel at peace and keep the proper balance in my life. A lot of times, I like to ask myself, *How can I accomplish the most good in my life? What choices can I make right now—ones that can really make a difference? Is there something important I can do today?* It doesn't matter where I am, if I'm on tour, on the road recording, at home with my family, visiting relatives, or at some type of an event, it still all boils down to trying to stay true to what I believe in at all times. Even if I don't feel like it. Even when it isn't popular or convenient. If I just worry about trying to do what's right, everything else seems to turn out fine.

I think deep down we all know what's *really* important in our lives; we just have to be honest enough with ourselves to face that truth.

Why do I bring this up? Well, a question I get a lot is "So, have you changed much since all this *Idol* stuff?" I understand why people might think that because of what has happened over the past several years of my life, I might have changed into someone else, someone who is unapproachable or thinks he is "better" than the "old me." But the truth is that there is no "old me." There's just the "me" that's always been here, and the "me" that I hope to keep bettering and improving as time goes on. When your life (for better or for worse) changes dramatically overnight, it's easy to lose sight of reality. So I think it's really important to do everything you possibly can to stay true to yourself.

One thing that always helps me with this is to remind myself that there are two kinds of success: success in the world's eyes and success in God's eyes. For me, success isn't based on fame or money or popularity. It has nothing to do with being on TV, traveling the world performing, or financial success. Those things are fun, and I enjoy them. But to me, the most important success is knowing that you are trying to do what is right and staying true and constant to your set of values. This is why I feel it is so important to trust your intuition and listen to your conscience.

The greatest joy and satisfaction I feel is from trying to simply do what is right, by listening to the promptings that come to me through the "Spirit." I believe everyone has a conscience, which is really the spirit of God that tries to teach us all what is right and wrong. It seems like when we learn how to listen to and follow our "conscience," which I believe to be the promptings from the Spirit, we feel truly happy. We make better decisions; we are less judgmental, more patient, more understanding, more caring, more loving; we are more sensitive to other people's feelings, all the attributes that I think make someone a great person. It can help us in all areas of our lives, with our work and school and developing our talents and being trustworthy, honest, and responsible—and all the things that make up a good character.

Keeping the Spirit close also helps us when we face challenges in life and gently pushes us to keep the proper perspective when things are uncertain or confusing. But most of all, it helps us with our most important relationships which for me, are those with my Heavenly Father, my family, and my friends.

It is also interesting to understand how the promptings of the Spirit work through other people as well. Remember what I told you about how I had been a Boy Scout growing up? Well, the greatest achievement you can accomplish as a Boy Scout is the rank of Eagle Scout. As I was so busy with touring and working on my album, I was only home for one or two days every couple of months or so, which made it impossible to even think about finishing the last few steps that I needed for my Eagle.

> ...it's really important to do everything that you possibly can to stay true to yourself...

But I had a great neighbor, Cal Madsen (who had gotten me into scouting to begin with), who saw me at church one Sunday and called me into his office. He's also the bishop of the Young Adult Singles ward. I hadn't seen him in a while, because I'd been so busy touring, and just hadn't been home long enough to even go to my own home church or really see any of my old neighbors and friends. I knew he'd ask me about scouting, because he always checks up on me and is the person who made sure I was progressing through the various scout ranks and getting the required merit badges I needed to get. He asked me how long I was home. I said, "I don't know? Three days or so?" I thought I'd be leaving the next Thursday or Friday to go to New York.

That was the window of opportunity Cal was looking for, so he suggested I do my Eagle Scout project in those three days. And, you know, although that whole thing had slipped onto the backburner after *American Idol*, I thought, *Why not?*

So things were set in motion. I got motivated. Yes. Me! Motivated. I called the parks and recreation department. I called my friends. I called my bishop, my grandpa, and a bunch of my neighbors. I got a pretty big group of people together and organized a tree planting service project at the Jordan River Parkway. My friends and neighbors and family took time out in the middle of a busy school and work day to shovel dirt and plant well more than one hundred trees to help me finish that one last requirement so I could get my Eagle. You had to finish everything before your eighteenth birthday and I was coming up on it soon, so this really was my last chance if I was going to actually achieve it. That's one thing I really like about where I live; there are lots of genuinely good people who listen to their conscience and like to do good things just because. They have really meant a lot to me.

So I got my Eagle Scout and *again* realized that there is something to be said about perseverance (on Cal's part probably more than my own), about not giving up, and not letting my music life get in the way of other things that are perhaps not as important to the "world," but are definitely important to me. Scouting is something that a boy begins at age twelve and goes until eighteen, but you have to finish your Eagle before you reach eighteen. It is one of the greatest programs for developing character and values in youth, the things that are rarely addressed these days it seems. It is a six-year potential journey in scouts, and I felt so proud to be able to accomplish that goal while being so busy with my new music career. I feel so blessed to have a family and community that encourage such activities. I believe a lot of what I learned there has prepared me for more important opportunities that will come later in my life.

I sincerely appreciate all of the amazing things that have happened to me over the past few years. I absolutely love singing and the opportunity it allows me to meet so many people and to share all those special feelings I've talked about earlier on, but I'm totally grateful every single day of my life for all the other less obvious blessings that have come my way. Just because I've been able to succeed as a singer doesn't mean I've changed what is most important to me, as I still feel that my true mission and measure of success is based on first trying to be a good person. And to be a good person, means you think about others and care about them, usually before you worry about yourself.

Without this, I don't think any amount of personal success can make life truly complete. For me, taking time out every day to ponder and pray is the best way to stay connected with our Heavenly Father. By being mindful of my values and keeping my spiritual beliefs close to my heart, I truly believe it helps me stay grounded and always respect the place from where my talents and successes spring. Yes, I've worked hard; and yes, I may have achieved a certain level of success—but I'm very clear about the fact that none of it would be worth it without doing the things that keep me close to God.

I've talked a lot about what it takes to stay on course, to stay positive and strong; and I've talked about faith as my main tool for being able to do so. But there are a number of other personal values that I've tried to stick to as I've gone through the ups and downs of my "insta-career" and all the chaos (good and bad) that came with it. They help me stay as true to myself as possible in a world that regularly asks us to compromise our integrity. I knew that I would need to arm myself with tools for staying true, and to this day I try to tap in to them regularly.

Perspective has played a major part. Although I had my dad with me during most of my musical experience, it was hard to be away from the rest of the family. Being away from my mother and siblings for so long made me miss them terribly, so my returns home are always charged with deep tenderness and so much love. I now see my time at home as a

Courtesy of Scott Allen

My dad has always encouraged me and supported me

treat, a bubble of total safety where I can be the David I've always been, temporarily removed from the demands of my career. I would even go as far as to say that before all of this, I may have taken some members of my family for granted. But today, being home with my family any night or day of the week feels like a total blessing, something I cherish and long for whenever I'm away.

Absence *does* make the heart grow fonder, which I was able to learn *only* from being away. Just being far from the people I love most gave me an entirely new perspective. I began to appreciate my siblings so much more, seeing them each shine with their own unique gifts, skills and passions. My new point of view has also helped me to see my parents for what they really are: supportive, encouraging, inspiring and basically the rocks that I will always lean on through good and bad experiences.

My father, for example, was always there for me. He was the one who really looked after me in this crazy time in my life and during this whole journey starting when I was very young. In this entertainment world of adults, it could be easy for a young, naive newcomer like myself to get manipulated and taken advantage of. But my dad was always looking out for me. He helped make sure that each decision we were faced with was made carefully, and he made sure to find people to be part of our "team," who would respect my values and make sure they didn't take advantage of my lack of experience. My dad is the one who has always understood me from the very beginning, and the reasons why I really wanted to sing and get into music in the first place. He helped me stay grounded when things got difficult. He was the one person who constantly kept this in mind despite the challenges surrounding me. He made sure that I always had what I needed and helped me feel prepared when I wasn't sure what I should do. He sacrificed a lot in order to help me have all the opportunities I've been able to experience so far.

I couldn't have accomplished any of what I've done without my dad, who was willing to give up so much of his own time and energy to make sure things would go as smoothly as possible for me. I know it wasn't easy for him, and I appreciate all he's gone through. To me he's been an example of how a father shows love to his son. His support has been unconditional and constant, and for that I am truly grateful.

As for my mom, she was a big part of my musical influence as well, but that's only touching the surface. She has always been a positive, loving role model not only to me, but also to all of my siblings equally. Her love of entertaining made singing and performing something extra-special in our home, but that wasn't nearly as important as the way she always took such good care of our family so unselfishly. Her zest for music was a constant, but I remember more of how she would get up every morning before school and fix us endless stacks of pancakes, French toast, and oatmeal. I spent much of my youth listening to my mom sing her heart out, and I know a lot of my inspiration also comes directly from her.

Courtesy of Lindsay Farnworth

Emotion is the driving force of all my shows

CHORDS OF STRENGTH

But as serious as I am about music, I'm just even more intent on making sure my family relationships and friendships are properly taken care of. These are the people who have loved me unconditionally, some ever since I was a little kid, since before I even knew that things like *American Idol* or *Star Search* existed. These are the people who believed in me when I didn't believe in myself. They are the ones who have always shown me respect for who I was, not for what I have accomplished. I feel like I have learned so much from my friends, and I take a lot of my cues directly from these people, who have not only been by my side as pals but also, in many ways, serve as role models for the kind of person I want to be. Some of my closest friends are so motivating in the way they live and the choices they make, and since I'm surrounded by the often superficial world of

I see it as my duty to give back whenever I can . . .

"the industry," it's always so refreshing for me to be able to come home to what's familiar, what's real.

Friends are the ones who will always have your back and their perspective on you doesn't change no matter what! They keep it simple, they keep it real and they keep it familiar. To me, that's priceless. They don't look at me just as a famous singer; they look at me as David.

I guess I see it as my duty to give back whenever I can, even if that means finding a minute here or a second there between meetings and appointments to make sure that the people in my world feel as loved and cared for as I always have. I feel that besides one's own sense of self-worth, the most powerful strength you can get is the love and support that someone else is willing to give you. There's nothing more empowering than knowing that someone else believes and has faith in you; especially when that someone is a person you love and respect, or who has always been a part of your life. In a way, it's almost like this type of strength is what makes the world go round, with all of us just trying to help one another out, a chain link of love that lets people shine. I don't think we can overstate how important love is—not romantic love necessarily, but instead true, pure, unconditional love. It's the stuff we're all made of when we're at our best, and the stuff we should all aim to cultivate throughout life.

Something else that always comes to mind when I think about what it takes to stay true is accepting that life isn't always pretty. Everyone knows that the human condition comes with all kinds of situations—the good, the bad and the ugly. Pain and hardship are almost impossible to avoid, right? For me, the best thing you can do when you feel pain or hardship is to use it as a tool for putting things into perspective. I guess because of how fast things have happened to me, people often say, "Oh, wow, it's like you're living a dream!" I understand why someone on the outside of my life might come to that conclusion, and this has been a dream for me; but I am human and I feel happiness and pain just like everyone else. Rather than feeling sorry for ourselves when the chips are down, we should take stock of the things that we actually feel happy and grateful for. If you think about it this way, pain can become like a barometer or a point of reference against which to measure the other aspects of your life that are going well. It's almost like without the darkness, we can't really appreciate the light.

For me, music is a way to communicate. It's a way of letting all that emotion out into the world, so that other people can hopefully relate in some way. I think when people relate to one another it creates this sense of community in the world.

If you always focus on what hasn't worked out the way you wanted, you miss out on seeing all those things that have. If you focus on the pain, you're not looking at the complete picture. Without the struggle, we can't really appreciate the joy when it comes. I could go on talking about pain in songs, but the thing that really drives me as a person and as a singer is the light in life, the high points. I know that the only way you can paint the complete picture of those high points is to also show and feel the low ones; but in the end, for me the joy always beats the pain. If I only ever looked at the bad things in life through my music, it would be such a plain and ugly picture. Whenever anything is too one dimensional, it's kind of boring. I mean, you don't want to look at a canvas that's painted completely gray, do you? Of course not! You want to see colors come alive; you want to see something happen; you want to see something dynamic with depth. You want to see all those beautiful, bright colors, but they will look that much more stunning if they're painted against the darker, dimmer colors that give a sense of contrast. It's everything together that makes the picture come to life. I think the same is true with music. In order to show people a sense of wholeness, I think it's really important to give them a wide range of emotion. In this way, I like to think of the songs I sing as symbolizing a slice of life—real life, with all the beauty and pain that's naturally built in to it.

To me, staying true is about knowing how to define success. The irony about that is that my success as a performer is not really what matters to me the most. It's totally the opposite: I try not to think about the fact that people like me, or enjoy the way that I sing. It's not about how far I've come, or what I've accomplished. It all goes back to the basic idea of sharing: sharing a moment with someone, sharing my passion, sharing a feeling that I may have experienced that maybe someone in my audience is going through right now. This is really at the heart of everything I stand for, and it's the most important thing to me in regard to my music. That's why I like to call my singing a gift and not a talent, because a gift is something that passes from one hand to the next, as a gesture of goodwill, as an act of compassion and love. "Talent" implies some degree of unique skill, whereas "gift" takes the simple description one step further and makes that talent something meaningful to share with the rest of the world. Talent mostly serves the person who has it—but a gift, by definition, is something special to give and receive. To me, this is the heart and soul of music.

Courtesy of Kim Meade

This is a show in Rockford, IL. I love how calm I look in this one

It's like if you heard a really funny joke, and never told it to anyone. Because when you hear that joke, you want to share it with someone, and it is actually the funniest when you hear someone else laugh at it, or when you get your chance to tell it for yourself. You want that other person to experience the punch line just like you did when you first heard it. It's like that with music, too. I naturally want to pass on what I felt when I first heard a song because to me that's what makes music so special: It's for everyone. It's ours.

If I had to break it all down to answer the question of how I stay true, it always goes back to the simple things: happiness, giving, loving, and sharing. Those are the things that are important, and everyone has different ways of finding them. You might think that sounds oversimplified, but I believe that when we simplify, we make life that much easier to handle. I think the way my life has unfolded has only helped me to

CHORDS OF STRENGTH

see those simple little things much more clearly. The whole fame and recognition game makes the really important things stand out in a way that shows me how meaningful they truly are. I have a deeper sense of appreciation for the small things in life that maybe I took for granted before all of this happened. I'm able to enjoy life's little treats with a new point of view, one that's largely shaped by gratitude.

I believe the only true measure of success is knowing that at each moment, you're living your life to its fullest. For me success is not measured by any single goal or milestone—but instead, by knowing that each second of life is precious and that no matter how high on the ladder you think you've climbed, there is always room for growth and progress. Once you let yourself believe that you've gotten to the top, you've lost sight of the real goal, which is to keep climbing no matter

Courtesy of Kim Meade

This is from one of my recent tours

what. And by climbing, I don't mean trying to outdo yourself with even more accomplishments. Instead, what I mean is that just when we think we have done something well, we should start looking at the other areas of our lives that also need our attention.

Again, if I take my own life as an example, it's important for me to be able to look at all the aspects of my world—not just music, singing and performing. After all, I am so much more than that. Before I was ever a singer, I was a son, a brother, a grandson, a nephew, a cousin, a friend—a person. Like everyone in the world, I come with many dimensions and I like to think that life is our chance to explore all of those dimensions and be the best we can in each one. Again, the moment we focus on only part of our existence, we lose the big picture; and the big picture is so much more interesting and complete than any one little thing in it.

> **Staying true is about knowing how to define success.**

Another critical lesson I've learned along the way is how to stick up for myself. Before all of this, I was just grateful to get the chance to sing, at any cost. Now that I've proven to myself that I can sing, and that I'm meant to, I feel a bit more confident to speak my mind when it comes to the kind of music I want to do. Maybe that's just part of growing up, or part of the learning curve that comes with anything. But I can tell you that it's totally empowering to know what you want and to be able to communicate it. I'm not saying that you should always think people are out to get you, but I have definitely learned how important it is to not be naive and to stand up for whatever your beliefs may be, whether it's about music, my personal beliefs or anything in between. Experience has taught me that all relationships, whether personal or professional, have to be about both parties helping one another—equally.

I know now that I can't just blindly accept what people tell me, and that I have to really think everything through and make choices that work for me. I'm not talking about being selfish—I'm talking about being honest with yourself about your need to feel good about whatever it is you are doing at any given time, and with a bit of maturity I've learned to step back and think about what works for me and what doesn't, without feeling bad about upsetting anyone or letting people down. I now realize that it would ultimately be much worse if I let myself down. After all, it is my life, and I should feel good about the decisions being made that will affect it. As I get older, I am clearer about the need to pay close attention to everything that's being asked of me, and all of the expectations that I'm supposed to meet. I think it's really important to set my own limits and create my own sense of expectations, because I'm the one who goes to bed at night and wakes up each morning with myself, so ultimately I'm the one responsible for my own peace of mind. As far as music goes, it's going to be my face on the cover of the album—so I better make sure I like how I am being represented. Better yet, I should be directly involved in deciding how to represent myself. This is also a major part of staying true.

the moment we focus on only part of our existence, we lose the big picture

It's about learning that sometimes you have to say no, and sometimes you have to be firm, and that it's okay. It's okay to not please everyone all the time. Sometimes you have to build the courage to say, "You know what? I would rather do it this way," or "Actually, I prefer this kind of direction," or "I'm sorry. That's just not who I am or what I want to say." Sometimes you have to be strong enough to simply say, "No, thanks. Not this time." I remember when it used to be really hard for me to do this, when I was afraid of letting anyone down. I just wanted to make people

Courtesy of Russell Hart

Courtesy of Christine Fitzsimons

Courtesy of Karen Ebert

Courtesy of Russell Hart

Courtesy of Joanna Manalo

Courtesy of Brandi Luff

Courtesy of Kim Meade

Courtesy of Alex Paisley

happy. But I guess life gradually teaches us the lessons that we're meant to learn, and in time, we figure out what we need in order to live happier. The funny thing about it is that people tend to show you more respect when you do stick up for yourself and speak your mind. They take you more seriously and begin to understand that your point of view matters and will ultimately create a better outcome.

One of the other lessons I have learned is that sometimes you have to pick your battles and that there's no use complaining about every little thing that comes up. Nothing is ever going to be perfect, so the best we can do is accept the fact that things take time and effort, and hopefully the end result is something that you can live with or better yet, be proud of. Music, like life, is a learning process. First you have to learn the melody; then you start memorizing the words, soon you are making the song your own, and before you know it, you're singing with pure, true emotion. But it doesn't happen overnight, and it takes all kinds of practice before you can actually feel good about yourself. I think the trick is to trust the process and enjoy the ride, not thinking about what the end result will be, but instead savoring the beauty of every little part along the way.

I have learned so much about myself over the years—good and bad. I've realized that the more I know about myself, the more I can live the rest of my life in a way that makes sense. Knowing myself well allows me to move forward with my strengths and weaknesses in check; it lets me get closer to what my ultimate goals really are. And beyond goals, knowing myself keeps me rooted in my truth. I understand now that even though your essence doesn't change, the things you go through as a person do change. So I think the key in life is to always be able to hold on to your essence no matter what happens.

In short, staying true is about staying grounded, and staying grounded is about never losing sight of who you really are.

CHORDS OF STRENGTH

DREAMING ON

"Success is not the key to happiness. Happiness is the key to success. If you love what you are doing, you will be successful."

—ALBERT SCHWEITZER

The future can be a scary thing, because it's something that's always left open for anything to happen. It's a total mystery. But at the same time, it's so exciting. Each decision we make can alter how our future will turn out, so how we end up in the future is really our decision. We never know what will be thrown at us, but it's up to each of us as to how we deal with whatever does come. No one else can decide that for us. While I might be wondering about what will happen down the road for me, and get nervous about it every now and then, I am also really hopeful for it because I know there will be so many windows of opportunity that can really change my life if I choose to take hold of them and not be afraid to go for it.

The proof is in
the pudding:
look at my smile!

Courtesy of Kim Meade

CHORDS OF STRENGTH

I think the word "success" is another thing that has been distorted by people. They say that you can't be happy and successful until the world knows who you are, or you no longer have to work hard for things. I really think that you become successful when you are on a path that you feel you are progressing on, and feel like you are accomplishing things that are worthwhile each day. Success to me is when you've found happiness. If you've reached "success" but still aren't happy, then have you really reached the point of true success? It doesn't make sense to me if you have one but not the other, because I think they go hand in hand. We should strive to succeed in finding happiness. Or maybe success means that you've worked hard, accomplished your goals, enjoy what you do, and have been satisfied with what you've done in your life. *Shouldn't that make you happy?*

I don't want to express myself creatively just for the sake of rubbing it in anyone's face, or having flashy things that get the most people's attention. I just want to be able to do well at what I love and feel good about, and to be respected for that.

I've been asked, "What will it take for me to always be happy?" I know how I would answer it: I would turn the question around and say that you should be asking yourself, "What can I do to make others happy?" I think that is the main point I want to get across to people reading this book. To me, the secret to happiness is that *it isn't all about YOU.* I am happy, but I try not to worry too much about things I want. If I just think about what I want, the type of feelings I get are not as fulfilling as the ones that come up when I am thinking about what I can do to help others feel happy. That way the flow isn't interrupted, it keeps going through me and on to other people. When I just think of myself, it stops with me and never seems to completely satisfy that inner desire to feel completely happy. That, to me, is that true key to happiness.

The other question I get a lot is, "Does music make me the happiest?" I would have to say that I have received a lot of joy and happiness from what I've been able to experience through music; it definitely means a lot to me. But happiness and music don't always go perfectly hand in hand. There are definitely times where music can cause a lot of pain, especially when you're already having a difficult time. Music is relatable, that's where the power is. I guess that's why spiritual music affects people the way it does. It's familiar and really draws us in, even though we may not understand exactly why.

So, looking forward, this takes me to another important question, which is, *what are my dreams*? I definitely have some that are music related and others that are not. I definitely have a dream of one day singing at the Olympics, an event that to me represents everything that I love about life in general: I like how it can bring millions or even possibly billions of people all over the world together. I love when people can share something like that in common and feel the joy that comes from such unity and oneness. I remember my first-ever concert was the closing ceremony of the 2002 Salt Lake City Olympics, which featured performances from artists such as *NSYNC, Christina Aguilera, Harry Connick Jr., and Sting. The levels of joy and celebration in the air were amazing. These types of unique occasions are so loaded already, and I love how music has the power to accentuate the experience with that much more spirit.

And as far as music goes, I look forward to being a part of it, whether it be as a writer, as a performer, or even as a listener. I really love songs that are about moving forward, about the power of progress and the ability to overcome; songs that really give people an idea, whether it's a better understanding of something in their lives, or a better understanding of me as a person. I just love the idea of sharing ideas through music, and I'm especially drawn to songs that have purpose, an angle. For me, the best songs are about getting through challenges: your basic "triumph of the human spirit" type of stuff, which is a common theme in music (and in life) that inspires me tremendously. Incredible music has been written about broken hearts or lost love, but it's so refreshing when you hear a song that has real depth of character.

I know I'm expected to sing and write songs about romance—but I also know that I like to sing songs that go beyond romance and that have more universal messages. Of course, we all want to be able to relate to the songs that we hear, but I think it's neat when those same songs are unique enough to stand on their own as different and distinct from what you might expect. Moving forward in my own musical development, this is the standard I'd like to set for myself.

I think for me, the bottom line is that I want to sing songs that make you feel good, songs that remind you about your right to choose happiness and finding the will to do so. I'm attracted to music that gets you thinking, that gets your mind moving in a more positive direction, music that stirs the soul somehow. I really do see each song as an empty canvas, as a moment of opportunity. With that in mind, my goal is to always paint a complete picture with my music, a picture that glows with color and dimension. I'm looking for movement in the songs that I sing, so that you actually go through something when you hear it, kind of like a life experience.

We never know what will be thrown at us, but it's up to each of us as to how we deal with whatever does come.

I'm sure that people have certain expectations of me, some because of the types of songs I performed when I was on *American Idol*; but I also know that I have my own expectations which may be different from what people have heard me perform in the past. To me, that means that my music should grow and change as I do, as part of a creative evolution that knows no limits. I want people to get a sense of what's going on in my mind, but even more than that, I want them to know what my emotions look like. Thoughts are one thing—but as I see it, the true beauty of human communication lies in the power of emotions. I feel that it's my job as an artist and a singer to communicate my perceptions through all the different colors of what I'm really like inside. So right now for me, music is the vehicle.

People are not born amazing singers. When I was six years old, I wasn't the best singer but I just may have been the most passionate! I loved it so much. When you have a passion for something and you work hard at it, that's when you start growing. That's when you start strengthening yourself as an artist.

Today, I love being busy. Sure, it can get stressful, but when you finish a task on your to-do list, it's always so gratifying. You think to yourself, "Man, I worked hard for this, and now I can say I did it." I have also learned that deadlines are excellent tools for me. The pressure gives me more of an appreciation for what I'm doing and forces me to be effective and stay focused.

But I don't feel that ultimate happiness can be achieved by finishing something. I like to believe that every time a milestone is reached, it's an open door for the next one to be tackled. I see my life as a progression of personal accomplishments that all tie together to show the truth. I love it when music makes a person say, "I get what that singer is feeling." When that comes through, I feel like I've done my job. And it has to do with several elements, a fine balance of things: the melodic flow of the song, its structure, its lyrics and, of course, the sentiment of the song. When all of these things come together to create a sense of connectivity between my audience and myself, I feel totally complete. Now that I have gotten to this level, I know it's my duty to work even harder to get to the next one, whatever that may be.

I think that the only way to be truly happy and satisfied with your life is to keep working and improving, because we are never perfect, and the only thing that really makes us feel accomplished in our lives is to keep growing and to progress. I think that's the best feeling. As for myself, I know there is still so much I need to learn.

Looking toward the future, I know I can't kid myself about my personal challenges. For example, one of my goals is to continue learning as much as I possibly can about songwriting. Though it's one of the scariest things for me, it's necessary for my shaping as an artist. Not to mention that without songwriters there would be no songs to sing! As a performer of songs, I feel I should understand the process from the beginning—to *participate* in the process. Songwriting is the new dimension for me, the next level. I've been able to feel good about songs I've been a part of writing in the past, whether on my own or ones I've been able to write with other great songwriters, but I just feel I have so much farther to go. I can really appreciate the idea that being able to create something is incredibly satisfying. You can look at it and say, "Wow, this is something I helped create. It came to life. It's from my soul."

Even though I am not wholly comfortable with this (yet), to get it, I'm going to do what I have always done in my relationship with music: I'm going to *listen and learn*. I have been listening practically since birth; and the learning has always come naturally as I was exposed to the musical library that basically has been such a big part of my life. The songs have became a part of me, so now I hope that I will be able to evolve into understanding it so well that I can also participate in its creation.

I've done it before so I feel I have the potential, so now I just need to improve my skill set—and that comes with experience, exposure and education. The old me would have probably been completely freaked out by the idea of having to master songwriting, which is totally different from just writing a song. Now I see it as a new horizon for me—I see it as potential growth. I'm being given the chance to take my love for music further, and to begin thinking about how I can define myself as an artist. *What mark do I want to leave? What is my message? What do I stand for? What is my sound?* These are huge questions, and the answers will color and shape my future as a singer, writer and interpreter.

I've learned that cowriting is a great way to get the creative juices cooking. As you throw ideas around with someone, you begin to tune into the different frequencies that are open to you, and each person seems to have their own set of frequencies, so it's always a unique experience to write with different combinations of writers. Sometimes, there is just one other person, and sometimes we have four or five people. It may sound like a lot, and occasionally there can be conflicts of opinion, but other times, something just clicks and things come out better or in a completely different direction than you could have ever expected. You forget about judging yourself because you're involved in a musical discussion with someone else in the room. Writing with other people is great because *anything* collaborative is great; it is multi-dimensional, rich and textured. I've been spending the past few months doing a lot of writing with different types of writers and producer— some in Hollywood, New York, and Nashville, and each one with a different angle on music and direction. So I'm never sure exactly what to expect. It's been an amazing experience so far, and I'm very happy with the type of music we've been able to come up with. It is very inspiring! When you're in a room with a gifted songwriter, you stop floundering in self-doubt—instead, you step up and perform because you are charged by their energy. *It really is contagious.* You just have to make yourself open to it.

Another personal goal is to learn how to play guitar better so I can use it both for writing as well as actually accompany myself when I perform. As a singer, your voice is your instrument, and even though I play some piano, I'm approaching guitar playing with the mind-set that even though I already know how to play something, I want to also have another palette to draw from musically. I can kind of compare it to the idea of learning a new language, just like I speak a little piano and I hope to be able to speak guitar soon.

And speaking of new languages, another cool way to expand my musical vocabulary is to actually sing in different languages. After all, I learned my first few words in Spanish as a kid and enjoyed singing songs from a French musical in a Cockney accent when I was six; and

TOP 5 ARTISTS

▶ **Natalie Cole** because she has this unique quality to her voice that's amazingly soothing and smooth. Maybe I love her because it is a voice that I have always been able to relate to and crosses a wide range of styles. When my aunt Char gave me her greatest hits CD one Christmas, I was obsessed and listened to it over and over. I could feel her feelings in the songs.

▶ **Eva Cassidy** because I don't think there is anyone who I've ever heard sing with more sensitivity and emotion than she does. You can feel her heart when she sings. The way I sang "Imagine" was very much inspired by the way she sings. I also included her version of "Fields of Gold" during my 2009 Winter Tour, which although it was written by Sting, it is her version that is magical to me, ever since I first heard it during the 2002 Winter Olympics.

▶ **Michael Jackson** because his songs are so catchy and he was such a gifted performer. It was always a show, and always so much fun to watch. He was truly THE greatest entertainer! There's a reason why everyone loved him and why he influenced so many people.

▶ **Natasha Beddingfield** because she dares to be herself. She's not afraid to show her personality in her songs. She has some SERIOUS chops!

▶ **Stevie Wonder** because you can feel his happiness when he sings, and you can see in his expressions how much he truly enjoys it. The runs and riffs that he does are always so clean that it always makes me think, Man, I want to sing like that. I want to enjoy singing the way he does.

both my parents speak fluent Spanish so I've always been exposed to that. In fact, on my Christmas album that came out in late 2009, I was able to sing in four different languages: English, Spanish, French and Latin. I know English and a fair amount of Spanish, but playing with words in French and Latin was a totally different challenge. It felt so good to be able to reach out to people all over the world, and to dive into those cultures momentarily through their languages. The world is so large yet so small.

As it is, getting this far along on my path has already helped me in so many ways. I am freer, less inhibited, less afraid, more comfortable. I have more energy as a person, so my performances are more energetic. I've learned to let loose a bit and have more fun onstage. I never imagined that I could feel so relaxed in front of so many people, and now that I perform all the time, I realize how far I have come in terms of conquering my shyness. I have become more comfortable as a communicator. I am a little better at looking at and listening to footage of myself and I'm way more relaxed in front of cameras. I even agreed to try out a little acting by being myself on *iCarly* and *Hannah Montana*! That was something I never imagined was going to be in my cards. But the universe works in mysterious ways, and our job is to trust it no matter the crazy and unforeseeable twists and turns.

I don't know if I'll ever completely come to terms with the idea of being a "pop star." First of all, to me, I'm not even in the same league as what I consider to be a pop star. I just want people to know that I am truly happy to be here, whatever "here" means! When I first heard someone refer to me that way, I was put off, thinking that it carried such negative connotations. But now, I have redefined what I think a pop star really is—and through this new perspective, I have more respect for the whole thing. A pop star is someone who works hard to communicate and share their talent with other people, and someone who is committed to improving and excelling at what they do. It is someone who consistently uses their God-given talent to work hard and progress.

Courtesy of Joanna Manalo

Sometimes you never know where the inspiration or feeling will come from

To get people to respect your music: I think that's really the goal. In general, the artists that I respect the most are the ones who cannot just sing songs in many different styles, but whose personality ties their body of work together. There is nothing more interesting than diversity and range; but to me, it's just that much cooler when within all that range there's the common denominator of the artist's unique personality and character.

I think Beyoncé is an example of "the ultimate pop star" and, of course, the king himself, Michael Jackson. I was performing at a show in New Jersey when I found out about his death. At first, I thought someone was making some kind of cruel joke. I thought it was an Internet rumor or there would be some other explanation that would account for this totally unbelievable piece of news. Michael was definitely always one of my major influences ("Man in the Mirror" is one of my favorite songs), and I think his love for music showed. You could see it when you watched him or listened to him; and you could always see his love of people. His spirit was sweet and sunny. I think he really understood what music could do for people. He communicated through his music and you could feel his love for people through it more than anything.

As I said, I strongly believe that fame brings with it the opportunity to help other people. You can use your name for the purpose of doing good, as opposed to just being tabloid material all the time. You can actually make a difference. I feel that all celebrities should take this responsibility seriously and take advantage of their position to spread positive messages. I hold this as a top priority as I move further along in my career; whatever "status" I have will be as much for others as it is for myself, because fame is nothing without generosity and kindness. I have been able to rally behind several great charities and it has been so rewarding to see how much my fans have also gotten involved. I'm amazed at the service and donations they have contributed to these causes like Rising Star Outreach, Make-a-Wish, MS Society, Do

Something.org, Stand UP for Cancer, Invisible Children, and the Haiti Disaster Relief efforts. I want to recognize the commitment and personal sacrifices that all the various fan sites make to respect and support me and the causes we are involved with. It makes me so proud to have fans who show through their enthusiasm and actions that they really want to give. It is the greatest way they can show their support of me, and I hope they all know how much I appreciate what they do. I was so honored to be a participant in the Haiti Telethon in Hollywood and then to be a part of the "We Are the World" ("*Somos el Mundo*") in Spanish in Miami, and to see all these performers who were willing to give of their time and status to help those in need. If I'm going to sacrifice my privacy to be in the public eye, let it be for a good cause such as these. Let any sense of fame that comes to me matter for these kinds of reasons.

Another part of my future without question is school. I don't want to be off the hook just because I had some amazing opportunities as a young person. Instead, I want to maximize those opportunities by committing myself to my development as a person. Education is definitely part of that agenda, and despite the crazy road trip that has become my life, I'm determined to find the balance somehow. I've been trying to do some schoolwork online, but it is really difficult when you are recording, rehearsing, and touring all at the same time. My intention is to work on finding this balance because I hope to go to college someday. I love the idea of studying philosophy, which has always been a subject that really interests me. Classes like that get your brain working and engage you to start thinking about the mysteries of life. Besides, I'm young, and while the singing thing is going wonderfully right now, you never know where life is going to take you. I want to be prepared for anything, and I definitely don't want to be one-dimensional. There are moments when I have the feeling that this has all been too much, too soon. Moments when I think to myself, *Am I really ready?* I don't kid myself about how young I am, and the fact that a life in entertainment is fast-paced, public and a lot of times stressful. Sometimes I ask myself if I really have what it takes. But in those moments, I remind myself that it's all about putting my trust in God. He wouldn't have given me this chance if I were not able to handle it despite how unready I really felt. He was the one who motivated me to audition in the first place and I don't think He would have allowed me to get this far if I wasn't capable of the challenges that surround it.

I figure each moment prepares you for the next one, so that by the time you reach the point in the future that you were so worried about, you are ready for it. This concept helps calm me down when I feel overwhelmed by what's ahead. I never think that I'm going to be ready for anything; but when it is right in front of me I usually end up surprising myself. If I have to leave you with one thing, it is that you should always be willing to follow your instincts. Our instincts, which you could also call our inner voice or our conscience, knows what's best for us, and tempted as we all tend to be to stifle that voice, we have to remember—*it knows*. It knows the deepest things about us. If I hadn't followed my instincts, I'd probably still be running sound tech at the Murray Amphitheater right now. Maybe many of us are discouraged from listening to our conscience because of the pressures we get from society to pursue other types of achievements. Everyone has their reasons for doing (or not doing) what they do. But it is now my deep belief that when you follow your gut, you almost always end up where you need to be. Deep inside, we know our own truths, so it is our job to pay attention to the rumblings of our soul.

As for myself, my conscience told me a profound truth about myself that essentially ignited me. It provided me with the answers when my life was all questions; it fueled me with faith when I wasn't sure what

> ... fame brings with it the opportunity to help other people.

Courtesy of Cassi Alligood

was best for me. It connected me with the parts of myself that would always matter most, and I know that it will continue to guide me as I move forward in my life. My conscience led me to give music another try and, in turn, has led me to great personal joy. I hope that my story has in some way inspired you to trust your own instincts, to follow your conscience, to have faith in yourself, so that you too can find joy and happiness.

And remember, even when you can't sing, you can always plant a tree. . . .

I was very fortunate to have been exposed to a wide variety of music and artists since I was young. This has definitely influenced my approach to singing and performing, as well as what I am now trying to get across in the songs I write. Every new song that I hear teaches me some unique lesson; it invites me to listen and learn from its structure and lyrics the emotional essence of the song. To this end, I have been a student of songs since I was quite young, reading several volumes of different Billboard books, trying to understand what songs were popular over the years, and more importantly, why they were popular.

There have been so many songs over the years that moved me intensely and they continue to so. I thought I would leave you with a list of some of my all-time favorites, a wide range of music that tells many different stories and communicates many kinds of feelings. Here they are:

SOME OF MY FAVORITE SONGS:

1. Joy Williams, "Every Moment." A really positive song from someone I really look up to as a person, not just as an artist.
2. Natasha Bedingfield, "These Words." This song inspired me to start writing. Natasha is willing to try new things and her lyrics are so relatable.
3. Tracy Chapman, "Fast Car." The first time I heard this song, I had goose bumps the entire time. After that, I couldn't stop listening to it. It's a song that lets me escape from everything.
4. Boston, "More Than a Feeling." I'm not really sure what I loved about this song so much, but it put me in a trance or something—I kept listening to it over and over. I still love it and it's one of my favorite songs.
5. Karen Clark-Sheard, "Higher Ground." A song that talks about moving forward in life and keeping hopes up. Her singing is amazing.
6. Kirk Franklin, "Imagine Me." Another song that helps to remind you of the important things in life and keeps you strong. This album was the first time I really started listening to Gospel music.
7. Manhattan Transfer, "Birdland." I love the harmonies in this song and how it's so unique.
8. John Mayer, "Dreaming with a Broken Heart." John Mayer is amazing because of the natural sense of groove that he brings

to each song. He always shows tremendous musicianship. His music is always interesting, never boring, and people really respect him as a musician. This song is about making a difference, and it happened to be my favorite song when I first auditioned for *Idol*. It was the first song that people heard me sing live on TV, so it will always have a special place in my heart.

9. Queen, "Bohemian Rhapsody." I don't really need to explain the greatness of this song! I'm one of the many who was greatly inspired by Queen.

10. Led Zeppelin, "Kashmir." This song showed me how much you could do with a song and that you don't have to follow the typical route for creating music.

11. Yes, "Roundabout." Another song I love for how different and creative it is. The chord progression in this song is so cool, and all its different sounds and changes make it totally unique. The song never gets boring, and it's eight minutes long!

12. Mariah Carey, "Butterfly." Simply one of the most beautiful songs I've ever heard.

13. Deborah Cox, "Nobody's Supposed to Be Here." I love the power and emotion in her voice.

14. Joni Mitchell, "Help Me." The first Joni Mitchell song I ever heard, and I listened to it nonstop.

15. Stevie Wonder, "Sir Duke." A great song explaining what music's all about, by a guy who represents what music's all about.

16. Michael Jackson, "Black or White" and "Man in the Mirror." Some of my favorite Michael Jackson songs. "Black or White" has such a catchy guitar riff, and it just makes me feel good. I think all of Michael's music makes you move in some way. He has without a doubt been one of my greatest influences, as I grew up listening to his music almost religiously.

17. Seal, "Waiting for You." He's such a brilliant songwriter, and I love the tone of his voice.

18. TLC, "Waterfalls." I listened to this song so much when I was a kid. I love it because it brings back memories of when I was younger. It's a song that makes you feel happy and a maybe a little sad, too. In general, the music of TLC showed this amazingly sweet groove that I loved for a good part of my childhood.

19. La India, *"Nunca Voy A Olvidarte."* Such a great cover because she really delivers these lyrics with so much passion and emotion. I also love the changes in the song, and how it captures the flavor essence of Latin American music.

20. Alanis Morissette, "Uninvited." This has a haunting melody that gives me goose bumps.

21. Selena, *"Amor Prohibido."* One of the first artists I ever liked listening to.

22. Idina Menzel and Kristin Chenoweth, "For Good." A song about appreciating how someone has changed your life.

23. Jackie Allen, "When Will I Ever Learn." I love this cover. It's always allowed me to calm down when things were crazy.

24. Kelly Rowland, "Stole." I love the blend of styles in the song, and the sad story.

25. Natalie Cole, "Pink Cadillac." The tone of Natalie's voice was so captivating to me when I was little, and this song in particular made me crazy. I would play it on repeat for months on end when I was nine or ten years old. I'm not sure what drew me to it, but I was obsessed. It's one of the first songs I liked that had kind of a soulful groove to it.

26. Imogen Heap, "Wait It Out" and "Hide and Seek." Such unique songs. I love anything Imogen sings, actually. She's never trying to be good or catchy—she simply tries to show emotion through her songs. She dares to be different, and you can hear it in every one of her songs. She *chooses* to be interesting, which to me is always the secret of amazing music. I love the pride she takes in being experimental.

27. Paul McCartney, "Maybe I'm Amazed." One of the best classic songs. Great emotion in his voice.

28. Eva Cassidy, "What a Wonderful World." One of the greatest songs *ever*. Eva has taught me so much about the power music has. I don't know of anyone who sings more sensitively. She brings out the emotion in both the lyric and the music.

29. Jason Mraz, "Beautiful Mess." He's a genius. His lyrics are just amazing, and I love his music.

30. U2, "One." I love how their songs are so big and powerful. So much passion in them.

31. Sara McLachlan, "Arms of the Angel." One of those songs I used to sing when I was nine or ten that allowed me to really escape, and be in a different place.

32. Tori Amos, "Silent All of These Years." I love how simple and beautiful this song is, allowing you to really pay attention to her story and what she has to say to people.

33. Dave Brubeck, "Take Five." I love the melody to this classic jazz song, which always gets stuck in my head.

34. Brandi Carlile, "The Story." She's such a powerful singer, she pours out her emotion throughout the whole song.

ACKNOWLEDGMENTS

I'D LIKE TO thank God for the many blessings He gives and continues to give. I've had so many opportunities that I never imagined could happen, and owe Him for the strength and the guidance. I hope this is another opportunity that I've taken advantage of to serve others and to glorify His name.

My mom and dad are the ones who have raised me and have really influenced all the experiences I've gone through in my life. They are the ones who have taught me how to handle it all, and I'm so grateful for their continued support.

I can't thank my brother and sisters enough for putting up with me all the time. Claudia, Daniel, Jazzy, and Amber: I know you guys deal with a lot but I appreciate how you never have changed the way you see me, for caring and for always being there.

I owe so much to the work that Monica Haim has put into this book. Thank you, Monica, for trying to be as understanding as you could with my stories and trying to preserve my character in here. I know it has been a lot of work for you, and I am glad I was able to have the opportunity of talking to you all these times and share these stories with you personally. Thanks for doing your best and putting so much effort into it.

I'd like to thank my publisher, Raymond Garcia, for going way beyond the call of duty to make sure I was happy with this book, as well as Tracy Bernstein, Kim Suarez, Kara Welsh, and everyone else at Penguin marketing, publicity, and sales.

I would also like to give my gratitude to "Maddy." You rock! Ha ha!

There are so many of my friends that have directed me to great experiences and wonderful moments in my life. I'm thankful for each of your contributions to my life. Some of them may have only been simple things, but they have been life changing and so influential. Thanks for continuing to teach me and share your advice with me.

I'd like to give a shout-out to my extended family, who were also a big part of raising me to become who I am today. My grandparents, my cousins, my aunts, my uncles, and all other family members who have been such a blessing in my life.

To all the people that I work with, I appreciate all the work you guys do! Thanks for encouraging me to do this project, and for making sure things run smoothly. Jared, Josh, Lauri, and the others who have helped with this book.

I'm so grateful to the fans who have allowed me to do music and continue my journey beyond what I ever thought I could do. This book is dedicated to you guys, and I hope by sharing these stories and thoughts with you that you will be able to grab and learn something from it. I hope that there is something in here for each one of you and that you will have a better understanding of why I am who I am.